LANGUAGE, BANANAS ᴀɴᴅ ᴅ...

For Annabel Cormack

Language, Bananas and Bonobos

Linguistic Problems, Puzzles and Polemics

Neil Smith

BLACKWELL
Publishers

First published 2002

2 4 6 8 10 9 7 5 3 1

Blackwell Publishers Ltd
108 Cowley Road
Oxford OX4 1JF
UK

Blackwell Publishers Inc.
350 Main Street
Malden, Massachusetts 02148
USA

British Library Cataloguing in Publication Data
A CIP catalogue record for this book is available from the British Library.

Library of Congress Cataloging-in-Publication Data has been applied for.

ISBN 0-631-22871-3 (hardback); 0-631-22872-1 (paperback)

This book is printed on acid-free paper.

Contents

Preface   vii

Prelude   1

1   How to Be the Centre of the Universe   3

Part I Problems   11

2   Tadoma   13
3   Putting a Banana in Your Ear   18
4   A Fragment of Genius   24
5   Colourful Language   28
6   The Structure of Noise   34
7   Dissociations   40

Part II Puzzles   47

8   Puzzle   49
9   PC   53
10 Acquired Whining   58
11 Godshit   63
12 The Golem   69
13 $ 75

Part III Polemics   81

14 Bonobos   83
15 Whales, Sunflowers and the Evolution of
    Language   89

16 Jackdaws, Sex and Language Acquisition   95
17 Does Chomsky Exist?   100
18 Relentless Jollity, Inexorable Logic and the
    Nature of Mind   105
19 Structural Eccentricities   110
20 The Velarity of Linguists   116

    Glossary   121
    References   134
    Index   146

Preface

I have spent much of the last forty years doing linguistics. It's been fun, and I'd like to share the enjoyment. The following essays are an attempt in that direction. They are lightly revised and updated versions of columns and reviews I have written over the last few years, mainly for the broadsheet *Glot International (GI)*, but also for a variety of other publications. My strategy, in so far as I have one, has been to take facts or observations that have struck me as inherently interesting or surprising, tease out their implications, and use them as a basis for drawing wider conclusions.

After an introductory Prelude, which sets linguistics at the meeting point of all human intellectual activities, I have divided the essays into three groups, of Problems, Puzzles and Polemics. In fact, all of them address issues which are problematic, puzzling and polemical in one way or another, so they can be read in almost any order. Most of them should be accessible to anyone prepared to go slowly and mull over the examples, but some of them – especially the last one in each section – presuppose knowledge or contain technicalities which may make them slightly less transparent. To help provide enlightenment, I have added a glossary of all the technical terms and technical interpretations of everyday words and expressions that I have used.

I am at heart a theoretical linguist, more particularly a linguist of the generative or Chomskyan tradition, and my prejudices will doubtless be apparent. However, my main prejudice is the conviction that explanation demands theory, and that some theory – almost *any* theory – is necessary if we are to make sense of the glorious riches of human language. Moreover, I am catholic in my interests, both factual and theoretical, and my instinct is to make connections between different facets of language and between language and other domains. As a result, I hope that even those who are not enamoured of current theory will find something to capture their interest. Another consequence of my desire to range widely is that I tend to stray outside the bounds of my own expertise, so I have doubtless made mistakes or unintentionally misrepresented some of the people or positions I cite. Corrections or other comments are always welcome.

The source of the original versions of the essays, together with additional notes and references, appears at the end of each chapter. Finding out more about any of the subjects addressed should be accordingly straightforward.

I am grateful to Stefanie Anyadi, Lisa Cheng, Annabel Cormack, David Crystal, Tami Kaplan, Fiona Sewell, Rint Sybesma, Ianthi Tsimpli, Hilary Wise, and all those whose work I have shamelessly plundered. They are not to be held responsible for what I have done with their suggestions.

As always, my greatest debt is to my family and my friends.

Prelude

1

How to Be the Centre of the Universe

Language makes us human.

Whatever we do, language is central to our lives, and the use of language underpins the study of every other discipline. Understanding language gives us insight into ourselves and a tool for the investigation of the rest of the universe. Proposing marriage, opposing globalization, composing a speech, all require the use of language; to buy a meal or sell a car involves communication, which is made possible by language; to be without language – as an infant, a foreigner or a stroke victim – is to be at a devastating disadvantage. Martians and dolphins, bonobos and bees, may be just as intelligent, cute, adept at social organization and morally worthwhile, but they don't share our language, they don't speak 'human'.

So what do you know, when you know a language, even though you may not have realized that you knew it? You know that *fish* is a word of English, and that *shif* and *shfi* are not. You also know that while *shif* might be a word of English, *shfi* couldn't be. How do you know that? You've probably never seen this sentence that you're reading before now, but you realize immediately that there is wrong something with it. How is that possible? You know that the sentence *my son has grown another foot* has all sorts of different meanings: he may be twelve inches taller, he may now have three legs, he may have succeeded in cultivating groups of toes in plant-pots, and on. You also know that some of these interpretations are rather unlikely to correspond to situations in the world we live in, but you none the less know that the sentence could be used appropriately to describe such situations if they ever did arise, or to relate a fairy story, or to describe a nightmare or a bad trip. How can you know such things about sounds, structures and senses with such certainty, even though they are not the sort of thing you're usually taught in school?

Linguistics, the scientific study of (human) language, provides answers to such questions and to innumerable others like them, giving us in the process both insight into one aspect of the human mind – the capacity for language – and a potential tool for helping those with a language problem. The capacity for language is universal: infants across the species have the same basic ability to acquire any language with which they are confronted, and to do so in the space of a few short years. Moreover, they do it in the same way, going through the same stages whether the language being learned is English or Welsh, Amharic or Zulu; whether it is spoken by hundreds of millions (like Chinese and English) or by a few dozen people in an African village. And all these languages appear to be equally effective in allowing their speakers to use them to think and communicate. There are no 'primitive' languages with only a few hundred words.

This universality has wider implications. Let's look at the diagram and begin to consider some of the interconnections between language and everything else. The claim may be contentious and the debate often obscure and ill-tempered, but universality is often cited as evidence that the ability for language is genetically determined: it is innate. Notions of innateness have been central to philosophical debate for centuries, and the most persuasive evidence, however you interpret it, comes from knowledge of language. If something is 'innate', it must be the property of a person, rather than of society as a whole, and in at least one framework (the Chomskyan one) the domain of linguistics is taken to be about the knowledge possessed by individuals, not (in the first instance) about the culture possessed by communities. On this interpretation, linguistics is a part of psychology – the

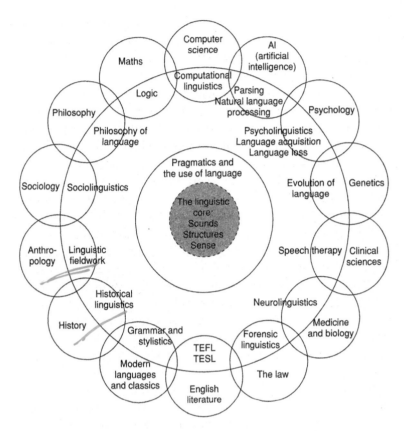

study of all forms of human behaviour; and psychology in turn is ultimately part of biology. This relationship of linguistics to the so-called life sciences has long been uncontroversial, but recent advances in neurology and imaging mean that at last we are able to provide evidence from studies of the brain for facts of language. On the basis of quite simple observations, it has been known for centuries that language is predominantly located in the left hemisphere. Physical functions on one side of the body are largely controlled by the opposite side of the brain: the left hemisphere is responsible for your right hand and foot, and the right hemisphere for your left hand and foot. So if you have a stroke in the left hemisphere, your right side is likely to be paralysed, while damage to the right hemisphere results in paralysis on the left. But damage to the left hemisphere typically has a further, even more devastating effect: you lose your language, suggesting that that is where language lives.

To date, the balance of explanation between the brain sciences and language – neurolinguistics, as it's called – leans more to linguistics than neurology, because linguists have theories of the structure of language which can sometimes be correlated with activity in a particular part of the brain, whereas neurologists don't (yet) have theories which will make detailed predictions for the linguists to test. Knowing that different kinds of electrical activity correlate with syntactic as opposed to semantic complexity, and that that activity takes place in the temporal lobe, doesn't tell us anything *linguistic* we didn't know before – that it's essential to distinguish syntax and semantics. Gradually, though, imaging studies are promising to answer substantive questions posed by linguists: for instance, are the two languages of bilinguals stored separately or together? The answer so far is not entirely clear (see Kim et al. 1997) but we can give a guarded 'yes'. The neurological connection is most clearly in evidence in the clinical sciences, where speech and language therapists can bring hope and improvement to the lives of those stricken by brain damage. The centrality of language to our lives is most obvious when we lose it, and only those who have direct experience of such loss appreciate the complexity and difficulty of the speech therapist's task.

This link to the clinical does not exhaust the domain of the speech sciences. Language and linguistics are central to such things as the automation of question-answering databases, to automatic (machine) translation, and to the whole domain of artificial intelligence: the attempt to model human mental functions with computers. AI has made huge progress in the last half-century, so that computers can now beat the world champion at chess, but getting a machine to simulate human *linguistic* abilities has proved the most intractable problem of all. The human mind is awesomely complex, and this is nowhere more apparent than in its capabilities in language. Progress in all these areas has relied heavily on increases in the power of computers, and, as one might expect, there is a flourishing enterprise in computational linguistics as well. This computational base has in turn been underpinned by the advances in mathematics which have taken place over the last fifty to sixty years and, with the cross-fertilization characteristic of developing academic fields, there has grown up a branch of mathematics devoted to the mathematical properties of different kinds of language (both artificial and natural).

Linguistics is not merely cognitive and computational; it also has a social, cultural and literary dimension. Most people first come to linguistics via the English language and its literature, and then discover in return that linguistics can answer question about these domains too: from the statistical properties of a Shakespearean (as opposed to a Baconian) text to the metrical properties of the iambic pentameter, and to notions of style and genre more generally. What is true of English is true of other languages, be these the dead classical languages of antiquity or the modern languages, Eastern and Western, which form the basis of many university courses. The teaching and learning of all these languages can benefit from the analytic insights of the linguist, whether the task is for a Japanese learner to master the use of the English definite article or the English learner to get to grips with the nuances of the Japanese honorific scale.

On the social side, linguistics has intimate connections with anthropology (indeed, it is sometimes described – for example, in the *Encyclopaedia Britannica* – as one constituent component of anthropology) and, of course with sociology. The tie here is with sociolinguistics, which can demonstrate correlations between particular features, like the pronunciation of 'r', or the use of constructions like '*John is stronger than what I am*', and particular geographical, generational or sociological variables. Like anthropologists and sociologists, linguists indulge in 'fieldwork', which can be in an English urban environment, as well as in the mountains of New Guinea. As a graduate student I spent a happy year living among the Nupe in a Nigerian village, assimilating their language and writing a grammar of it for my PhD thesis.

There are even connections with the law. Linguists are more and more frequently called upon to give expert evidence in court: to compare the acoustic properties of a suspect's speech with those of a tape recording, or to judge whether particular syntactic constructions are characteristic of one ethnic group rather than another. It is common in this area to hear claims made which are more ambitious than they are scientifically substantiated; and it falls to the forensic linguist to pour cold water on them. And the laws of libel and slander are almost unthinkable without having recourse to language.

We have almost come full circle, but there remains the historical dimension. This could be viewed as cross-cutting almost all the others, but there are two areas where it is especially prominent. The first of these is historical linguistics, pursued either for its own sake as giving an insight into how and why languages can change, or as a tool for the investigation of historical documents, from the decipherment of ancient scripts like Linear B or Mayan hieroglyphics, to the analysis of Doomsday Book or Magna Carta. The second is as a handmaid of archaeology, where linguistics can provide evidence about population movements and ethnic relationships. A sad offshoot of the historical side is the study of language death: languages die (or get killed), and with the increasing encroachment of English, Chinese and Spanish as world languages, more and more languages are dying, with serious implications for the human condition. And, finally, there is the evolutionary angle: the emergence in prehistoric times of language in humans. This is currently a growth industry, raising innumerable questions about our relatedness to other species, as well as whether this emergence accords with Darwinian theory or raises problems of a new kind.

All the foregoing seem to bear out the claim that language is central to everything we do, not just in the obvious sense that we couldn't do our physics or chemistry without using language, but in the more interesting sense that language has close intellectual bonds with almost every discipline one can think of. It is important in all this, however, to remember that we need to distinguish knowledge of language (the initial domain of linguistic inquiry) from the use of that knowledge in particular areas. Most of the following essays concentrate on our core knowledge, but almost all of them branch out into one or another of the areas mentioned here. In doing so they regularly appeal to another discipline that I've kept under cover until now: pragmatics – the study of language use – which forms a bridge between our core knowledge and our deployment of it elsewhere.

pragmatics

Pragmatics has its own theories and principles, as can be seen from the consideration of one or two typical examples. Given an exchange between host and guest like *'Would you like some coffee?'* – *'Coffee would keep me awake'*, we all know what the second sentence *means*, but we also know what it *suggests*: that the guest is declining the offer of coffee. Similarly, if I (truthfully) tell you that *'My first wife gave me this watch'* there is a strong implication that I have been married more than once. But of course the only wife I have ever had is also my first wife, misleading though this characterization may be. These implicit suggestions have the interesting property that they can be cancelled in the right context: you know I want to stay awake, so I'll accept the coffee; we have all been comparing gifts from our spouses and I am known to be the only one to have had but one, so I'm taken to be joking about 'my first wife'. Crucially, however, these interpretations depend on our strictly linguistic knowledge, with the implications going beyond that knowledge, and presupposing more general principles of rationality and cooperation. Here the central notion is 'relevance', by reference to which we arrive at the meaning intended as well as the purely linguistic meaning. But we can arrive at it only because we have knowledge of language.

So if you want to be the centre of the universe, become a linguist. The worst that can happen to you is that people will ask how many languages you speak.

Note

An early version of this essay and the accompanying diagram appeared (anonymously) in an undated edition of *UCL Arts* around 1990.

For more information on each of the domains which intersect with language the best source of first resort is Crystal (1997). Many of the issues raised here are discussed in Smith (1999) and several of the essays which follow. More specific references include: philosophy of language: Guttenplan (1994); Lamarque (1997). Mathematical linguistics: Partee et al. (1993). Computational linguistics: Cole et al. (1995). Natural language processing: Crocker et al. (2000); Fodor and Ferreira (1998); Cole et al. (1997); Brown and Hagoort (1999). Psycholinguistics: Aitchison (1998); Harley (1996); Napoli and Kegl (1991). Clinical linguistics: Crystal (1981); Grunwell (1987); Blanken et al. (1993). Speech and language therapy: Crystal (1982). Neurolinguistics: Gazzaniga (2000); Brown and Hagoort (1999); Chomsky (1999b); for an extreme view on the irrelevance of localization, see Fodor (1999). The law and forensic linguistics: Baldwin and French (1990); Pullum (1985). Applied linguistics (especially TEFL and TESL): Johnson and Johnson (1998). Literature, metrics and stylistics: Fabb (1997); Fowler (1996). Historical linguistics: McMahon (1994); Hock (1991); (on language death: Crystal 2000; Smith 2001). Anthropological linguistics and fieldwork: Duranti (1997); Payne (1997); Smith (1964). Sociolinguistics: Coulmas (1997); Hudson (1996). Pragmatics: Kasher (1998); Sperber and Wilson (1995).

Part I

Problems

2

Tadoma

Imagine a baby, born blind. What effect does blindness have on its ability to learn its first language? The answer, provided in elegant work by Landau and Gleitman (1985), is essentially none. Congenitally blind children learn to use the vocabulary of sight with remarkable ease and consistency, differentiating 'look' and 'see', 'see' and 'touch' – both in their own actions and in their reactions to others – in ways that surprise even their parents. More impressively still, these children are able to learn the appropriate use of colour terminology, predicating 'green' (and indeed 'colourless') only of concrete objects and never of ideas. Language acquisition, perfect language acquisition, is more resilient than the British empiricists (especially Locke) and common sense would have us believe.

Imagine another baby, born deaf. What effect does deafness have on *its* ability to learn its first language? Here the answer is slightly more complex. If the parents bring it up to learn only a spoken language the effect of deafness is characteristically catastrophic: the child may end up isolated and speechless. In fact, it is worse than that: the child will be not just speechless but languageless, a grim fate. If, however, the baby is born to deaf parents, in particular deaf parents who communicate in Sign Language, the prospects are dramatically better. It is now a truism that Sign Languages have as great expressive power as spoken languages (see e.g. Sutton-Spence and Woll 1999); they are just another form of 'human'. Apart from minor idiosyncrasies of vocabulary, whatever you can say in your language, I can say in mine, and vice versa, irrespective of whether the languages are signed or spoken. Deaf children learning Sign as their first language are in no way disadvantaged vis-à-vis their hearing contemporaries. All of them end up with a vehicle whose power for representing and communicating thought are completely comparable. Deafness does not have to be the handicap the hearing community sometimes makes it.

The superiority of signing over silence has been emphatically highlighted in work by Rachel Mayberry. She demonstrates (1993) that people who learn ASL (American Sign Language) as a *second* language (after going deaf in childhood) have a better mastery of it than people who learn it as a *first* language at exactly the same age. The possession of the first language, in this case spoken English, makes possible a mastery of ASL which is on a par with that of native signers who learn to sign from birth. Again, perfect language acquisition is seemingly impervious to the effects of what might appear to be a devastating impediment.

Imagine a third baby, born both blind and deaf. What hope does *it* have of learning a language, either signed or spoken, and thereby gaining access to the world of its parents and peers? The answer is rather pessimistic. Such double incapacity at birth typically leads to the severest, and permanent, deprivation. But the crucial words are 'at birth'. People, like Helen Keller, who have gone deaf and blind a year or two *after* birth are in some cases able to achieve truly remarkable mastery of language: mastery on a par with that of 'normal' speakers and signers. Keller's (1903) achievement was made possible by Anne Sullivan devotedly spelling words in her hand. In other cases, the secret is Tadoma.

In an inspiring article, Carol Chomsky (1986) describes the case of three people who were left deaf and blind as a result of spinal meningitis at the ages of 19 months, 20 months and 7 years, but who none the less developed a system of language and communication which put them within normal limits on a wide range of linguistic tests. It is hard to imagine not succumbing to despair in such a situation, and equally hard to think how people whose major difficulty is finding each other might learn to communicate. Yet, in the absence of both the visual and auditory modalities, people can learn language through the medium of touch.

Tadoma was invented by Hofgaard in Norway over a hundred years ago and was named some thirty or forty years later after two deaf–blind children 'Tad' and 'Oma', on whom it was used in the USA (Reed et al. 1985). It is a method of teaching speech and speech-reading based solely on vibrotactile information. By putting his or her hand on the face and neck of the speaker a deaf–blind person can monitor the articulatory motions associated with normal speech production. This provides information about laryngeal vibration (relevant for voicing distinctions), air-flow (relevant for distinctions of manner and place), lip movement (relevant for contrasts of roundedness) and jaw movements (relevant for some vowel distinctions). This is so much information that an experienced Tadoma user can interpret speech at a rate – and over a range – which approximates normality, and can do so with speakers who are entirely untrained.

In recent extensions of the method (Reed et al. 1995), Tadoma has also been modified to enable people to interpret ASL kinaesthetically: instead of holding the speaker's face the subject touches his or her hands, with the result that the speaker and the subject can establish an effective means of communication. Moreover, in a remarkable demonstration of human powers of integration, subjects appear to be able to interpret supplementary stimuli provided from an electro-palatograph. An artificial palate is fitted to the speaker, and information about tongue height (the hardest kind of phonological information for Tadoma users to identify) is fed via a microcomputer to a tactile display. An array of small rods is driven by piezo-electric vibrators to stimulate the index finger (or, less successfully, the abdomen) of the receiving subject, at the same time as he or she is holding the speaker's face (Reed et al. 1992). With this added refinement discrimination of phonological contrasts is close to perfection.

The linguistic abilities provided by Tadoma are rich. Phonologically, they include the discrimination of minimal sets such as 'hid', 'heed', 'had', 'hod', 'head' etc. Lexically, they include appropriate definitions of words like 'sentence', glossed by one user as: 'complete group of words written in one sentence; a judge gives a sentence'; and the correct differentiation of examples like 'see', 'gaze' and 'dazzle'. Most impressively, the abilities extend to the mastery of syntactic contrasts of considerable subtlety. The most experienced user (LD), who went deaf–blind at 19 months, not only handled negation, conjunction, pronominalization and a variety of other construction types successfully, but he also responded to the stimulus 'They are moving sidewalks' with: 'Means two things. People are moving sidewalks, or it could mean they are conveyor sidewalks. The sidewalks are moving.' He also provided systematic evidence of having intuitions of (semantic) ill-formedness: he rejected '*This math problem is not as hard as that rock' on the grounds that 'A rock is hard to knock, to touch. Math is hard in the head.' (An asterisk (*) is conventionally used by linguists to indicate that a sentence is ungrammatical.)

LD's linguistic ability is not perfect. He was unable to explain or identify the semantic difference associated with the choice of article in examples like 'Maggie looked at *the/a* puppy at Peter's Pet Shop, but later she decided not to buy *a/ the* puppy'; and he is insensitive among other things to intonation, to tag questions, and to exceptional 'control' structures, of the kind exemplified by 'tell' and 'promise'. But his linguistic prowess gives him sufficient independence to enable him to make his own way from out of town to the laboratory at MIT (the Massachusetts Institute of Technology in Boston), armed only with a card which explains his condition and solicits permission to let him touch another person's face so they can communicate.

It is worth pondering on this triumph of the will over adversity. It is significant that, like Helen Keller, LD and other successful users of Tadoma had been exposed to normal language before their illness. It is equally significant that all had been given dedicated one-to-one instruction for several hours a day over a period of many years. What is most striking, however, is the resilience of the human language faculty. In conditions where it would be hard to think of a much more impoverished stimulus, the mind/brain can still develop a system sufficient to facilitate thought and liberate communication.

Note

This essay first appeared in 1996 in *GI* 2,3:5. Work on Tadoma continues at the Research Laboratory of Electronics at MIT; see their Progress Reports.

3

Putting a Banana in Your Ear

[handwritten: Autist possess Theory of Mind]

Communication relies on sophisticated guesswork. Such guess-work presupposes that you are able to work out what your interlocutor has in mind. Hearing 'It's your turn', you might either reach for the dice or kiss the hostess, depending on your interpretation of the speaker's intention in the particular context. So much is simple and straightforward, though devising a theory that makes the right predictions is scarcely trivial, and it is one of the achievements of Relevance Theory (Sperber and Wilson 1995) that it has made a start on this enterprise.

But suppose you are incapable of entertaining the notion that other people *have* minds. Understanding what they are doing and reacting appropriately to what they are saying become problems of awesome complexity. This is precisely the position in which autistic subjects find themselves. A widely accepted current view (see Frith 1989 for an accessible and authoritative overview) is that the condition underlying the unresponsive self-absorption of autism is a defective 'Theory of Mind': that is, autists are unable to comprehend that other people have minds, and hence have a point of view, distinct from their own.

This inability can be most strikingly demonstrated by using the 'Sally-Anne' test, so called because the earliest version involved two protagonists, 'Sally' and 'Anne'. While the subject (Sally) and an observer (Anne) are both watching, the experimenter 'hides' an object, say a key, in position X. Anne is then sent out of the room and the key is removed to a new hiding-place, Y. Sally is now asked where Anne will look for the key when she returns. Normal subjects, including children from the age of 4, say position X; autistic subjects consistently say Y. The idea is that their absent or defective 'Theory of Mind module' renders them unable to impute a false belief to others. They *know* that the key is in position Y, and are hence incapable of ascribing to another mind the false belief that it is in position X.

A second simple experiment reinforces the same conclusion. Take a Smarties tube (this is a well-known kind of chocolate sweet, not an underground train full of academics), surreptitiously replace the sweets with a pencil, and ask the subject what is in it. The response from all subjects will, of course, be 'Smarties', until the tube is opened to reveal the pencil. Next, close the tube again and ask the subject what her or his friend will think is in it. The normal response is again 'Smarties'. The autistic response is 'a pencil' (or whatever happens to have been put in the tube), as autists cannot entertain the idea that anyone could have a mental representation of the world distinct from the real state of affairs.

For the last several years Ianthi Tsimpli and I (see Smith and Tsimpli 1995 and references therein) have been studying a unique individual, Christopher, who has some autistic characteristics. He was born in January 1962, and lives in sheltered accommodation because he is unable to look after himself. What is most striking about him is the mismatch between his verbal and non-verbal abilities. He has difficulty finding his way around; he has poor hand–eye coordination, so that everyday tasks like shaving or doing up buttons are a burdensome chore; he cannot devise a winning (or non-losing) strategy for noughts and crosses (tic-tac-toe); he fails Piagetian number conservation tasks; but he can read, write, speak, understand and translate some twenty or so languages. Christopher is a *savant*, someone who has an island of remarkable talent in a sea of disability. Most such savants have only limited language, their talent being musical, artistic or mathematical, as in the case of calendrical calculators (see the glossary) or the hero of *Rainman*. Christopher is unique precisely because his talent is linguistic.

Christopher's native language is (British) English, of which he has essentially perfect knowledge. We have subjected him to innumerable grammaticality judgement tasks, in which he has to indicate whether a particular sentence is 'good' or 'bad', or provide better versions of examples he finds unacceptable in any way, or select his preferred form in forced-choice tests. On the basis of such tests, it is clear that he has normal intuitions about a wide range of constructions from reflexives to relative clauses, from polarity items to parasitic gaps. Only phenomena like topicalization and focusing, which we argue involve non-linguistic as well as linguistic competence, cause him difficulty. In his other, 'second', languages he shows a marked asymmetry between different kinds of knowledge. His mastery of morphological and lexical material is stunningly good: he has a remarkable vocabulary in languages as diverse as Hindi and Polish, Turkish and Modern Greek; and he internalizes morphological paradigms with enviable facility, producing plausible, and sometimes even over-generalized, patterns with great consistency. In syntax, by contrast, all his languages appear to be filtered through English. Although he has mastered the possibility of having a 'null subject' in pro-drop languages such as Berber, Greek, Italian and Spanish, other properties associated with the 'pro-drop parameter' elicit systematic mistakes. For instance, in Christopher's production data, *that*-trace and wh-island effects regularly show up where they don't in those same languages.

Despite the wealth of linguistic material at his disposal, Christopher's use of his various languages is inhibited by the fact that, like many savants, he shows some signs of autism. For instance, he fails the Sally-Anne test but (sometimes) passes the Smarties test; an asymmetry which gives evidence of some normal and some autistic behaviour. It is worth emphasizing that such dissociation of responses suggests that autism itself is not a unitary phenomenon, but even 'partial autism' indicates that there is some defect in his Theory of Mind; some inability to represent the ideas of others the way we do. Apart from his diffidence in conversation, marked by a general tendency to monosyllabicity and a reliance on uttering rehearsed sequences of sentences, his difficulty is reflected in the fact that for Christopher translation is not a communicative enterprise but an automaton-like activity which proceeds largely independently of coherence and cohesion.

A corollary of the inability to impute false belief to others is a problem with pretence. Christopher is totally truthful and totally literal. He has great difficulty in understanding irony, metaphor, metalinguistic negation, rhetorical questions and jokes: all those areas of language use which involve some kind of metarepresentational ability. Accordingly, he cannot easily pretend to be what he is not, or understand such pretence in others. We were given a striking example of this while we were conducting experiments to work out precisely why his behaviour on different tests of autistic behaviour was asymmetric (see Tsimpli and Smith 1995 for discussion). The conversation went as follows:

Neil	(*picking up a banana*) I'm going to ring up Ianthi with this. Hello, can you hear me?
Ianthi	Shall I pick it up?
Christopher	Joke.
. . .	
Neil	What was I doing?
Christopher	Putting a banana in your ear.
Neil	Why was I doing that?
Christopher	I dunno.

Christopher's initial response, delivered totally deadpan, shows clearly that he recognized the abnormality of the situation, and had assimilated it to the category of jokes, a category with which he is familiar but of which he has no understanding.

His further responses show equally clearly that he had no real inkling of what was going on, and it was only after repeated prompting that he suggested the banana was a pretend telephone.

It is striking that by the age of 3 children have mastered pretend play of this kind, and as a child Christopher is reported as having indulged in pretend play himself. Yet interpreting the anomalous behaviour of normally sane linguists was initially beyond him. The task is deceptively simple, but to react appropriately Christopher had to work out not only what we were doing, something which occasioned him no difficulty whatsoever, but also what we had in mind in doing it. For five years we had met him regularly, talked to him in a range of languages, carried out innumerable tests, both linguistic and psychological, and generally behaved in a manner that had become reassuringly predictable. Suddenly he was confronted with behaviour that for him must have seemed bizarre.

Imagine the problems for someone who is isolated in this way inside his or her own world. Every act of communication requires not only a process of linguistic decoding, but also an attempt to interpret that decoded representation into something that will make possible an appropriate response, either verbal or actional. Christopher's position is better than that of typical autistic subjects. His linguistic talent is such that he can interact dramatically more with other people, and in a wider range of languages, than the archetypal autist. Moreover, his sheltered life, enhanced by the love and attention of his family, ensures that he has the maximum opportunity to benefit from such interactions. But even Christopher has serious difficulties in really understanding *why* what is going on is going on. He is restricted to the literal, to a single – real – state of affairs; but language use is rarely literal, because language reflects; and enables us to reflect on, the multiplicity of possible worlds we can imagine. To be restricted in this way is to be deprived of one of the main fruits of the human intellect. Remember Christopher next time you pick up a banana, or a telephone.

Note

This was the first in a series of columns for *Glot International*, and appeared in 1996 (*GI* 2,1/2:28). It was written jointly with Ianthi Tsimpli. The current stage of our project on Christopher (generously funded by the Leverhulme Trust, under grant F.134AS) involves teaching him British Sign Language (BSL), the language of the deaf community of Great Britain. See Morgan et al. (in press). For more on Christopher, see also chapters 4 and 16 below.

4

A Fragment of Genius

Are you intelligent? Since you are reading this book, you probably do consider yourself intelligent, even if not in quite so abrupt a fashion. But what is the basis for that judgement? Being good at history is no guarantee that one will shine at algebra, but it is a commonplace of the academic world that success in one area is a good predictor of success in others, and it is intelligence that is deemed to underlie success. Indeed the rationale behind ascribing people an IQ is that intellectual and other abilities tend to cluster. That one may wish to distinguish verbal and non-verbal intelligence is not taken to detract from the value of the measure: people are still intelligent or not.

Christopher (see chapter 3) makes any such assumption problematic. Now in his late thirties, he lives in sheltered accommodation because he can't look after himself; he has a severe limb apraxia which makes tasks like hanging a cup on a hook a tiresome chore; he has difficulty finding his way around; and he has some of the characteristics of mild autism. More strikingly, he usually fails to 'conserve number', a task which most 5-year-olds can do. We asked him to judge whether two wires contained the same number of beads, when these were, first, aligned so that the beads on the two wires were identically positioned, and, second, arranged so that the beads on one wire were spread out to form a longer line than those on the other. Christopher consistently claimed that whichever wire the beads were more extensively spread out on contained more items than the other. Yet Christopher can read, write, translate and communicate with varying degrees of fluency in some twenty or so languages. Christopher is a *savant*: someone with general disability but with 'fragments of genius', in Howe's (1989) felicitous phrase.

Is Christopher intelligent? On different IQ tests he scores anything from 40 to over 120: from the severely retarded to good undergraduate standard. He is not proficient at noughts and crosses, but he can translate from Portuguese to Polish. On holiday in Mallorca he kept getting lost, but acted as an enthusiastic and much appreciated interpreter between Spanish and German for some of his fellow tourists. He cannot impute 'false belief' to others (and does not lie himself), but he has a phenomenal vocabulary. Asking whether he is intelligent is not a sensible question. One thing Christopher makes clear is that intelligence is not a unitary notion.

His case casts light on other issues in linguistics and psychology, as well as on the theory of intelligence. After working with him for over a decade, it has become clear that he can provide evidence for the nature of everyone's knowledge of language, and for the structure of the human mind in general.

Although it was his prodigious polyglot talent that first brought Christopher to our attention, there is a striking mismatch between his ability in English and his proficiency in his other languages. His knowledge of English is just like that of other native speakers. Even though his own speech tends to the laconic, he has normal intuitions over the whole range of English sentence structure. He not only corrects simple mistakes of agreement and word order, but reacts appropriately to contrasts as subtle as that between the acceptable 'parasitic gap' *Which books did you throw away without looking at?* and the questionable *Which books did you throw away without looking at them?*

When it comes to his fifteen or twenty 'second' languages, the situation is rather different. First, his fluency varies from language to language: his French, German, Greek, Hindi, Italian,

Polish and Spanish, for instance, are probably much better than his Danish, Finnish, Norwegian, Russian, Swedish, Turkish and Welsh. I say 'probably' because we haven't tested him on all these languages recently and he may well have made unexpected progress through his interactions with people at his home. For the last couple of years he has been learning British Sign Language, and his fluency in that is increasing steadily.

In syntax his abilities are less striking. Although he can translate and communicate with some facility, he makes many mistakes, seeming to filter all his languages through English. He can cope with differences of the kind seen in the contrast between English *She read the book* and Spanish *leyo el libro*, where Spanish can, but English cannot, leave out the subject pronoun (Spanish is a 'pro-drop' language); but he consistently fails to judge correctly sentences like *Quien dijo que leyo el libro?* (literally: 'Who did she say that read the book?'), presumably because the 'that' in the English translation renders it ungrammatical.

Why should there be this double mismatch between his first and second languages on the one hand, and between the lexicon and the syntax on the other? Chomsky's theory of language provides at least partial answers, and hence Christopher's case lends some support to Chomsky's position. For Chomsky, the acquisition of our first language consists mainly in fixing the parameters of Universal Grammar (UG). We are born knowing the full range of possibilities provided by the world's languages, and our task is to select the grammar for the one we are exposed to. Once the parameters are set, we can absorb new words, but our syntax is fixed. Christopher's English is normal: he acquired his first language in the usual deterministic fashion but, despite his obsession with other languages, his learning of them is different.

That UG is still operative, in his case as in that of everyone else, was shown when we taught him and a group of undergraduates an invented language whose rules deviated from those made available by linguistic theory. We hypothesized that if we made up constructions which diverged from what is possible in human languages, Christopher should be unable to learn them, whereas the undergraduate controls should be able to use their non-linguistic abilities to solve the problem by raw intelligence. Our predictions were generally borne out, with the added twist that, when we invented a construction in which the subjects had to count words, not even the students could cope. More precisely, they couldn't cope until they were explicitly told to solve it as a puzzle; as long as they were engaging just their language faculty, structure-independent operations were ruled out.

Christopher's case shows a number of things: it indicates that Chomsky's theory of grammar is well supported; it provides evidence for a modular view of the mind; and it also shows that assigning someone a single IQ is silly.

Note

A shorter, and editorially rather corrupted, version of this essay, written jointly with Ianthi Tsimpli, appeared under the title 'Shards of genius' in the *Times Higher Education Supplement* of 29 March 1996. We were taken to task for the final remark (IQ is silly) on the grounds that IQ is, by definition, an index of intellectual capacity underlying a range of cognitive tasks. It still seems to me that such a measure is probably both silly and potentially pernicious, but there is a mass of research that either side in the debate can appeal to; see e.g. Duncan et al. (2000); Sternberg (2000).

5

Colourful Language

A noir, E blanc, I rouge, U vert, O bleu . . .
(A black, E white, I red, U green, O blue . . .)

Some people appear to have their perceptual wires crossed. Musicians sometimes report that they experience coloured music, with different notes and instruments having their own hues; a few people have tactile taste and coloured smell; and poets not infrequently associate colours with particular words or sound, as witness Rimbaud's poem 'Voyelles' ('Vowels'), whose opening line I have used as an epigraph.

Synaesthesia has been known for a long time, but recent experiments (Motluk 1995) have shown that the phenomenon is not due to the over-heated imagination of unreliable poets but that the experiences are consistent, reproducible, commoner in women than men and probably inherited. This suggests intriguing questions about universals, about the relation between mind and language, and about the structure of our cognitive capacities more generally. The issues are particularly relevant to modularity (in the sense of Fodor 1983) and the relation between 'input systems' and the 'central system'.

It is a truism that all languages have much the same expressive power: the richness and complexity of Universal Grammar (UG) guarantees that whatever you can say in your language I can say in mine and vice versa. Until, of course, it comes to technical vocabulary. The scientifically illiterate would probably have some difficulty with 'quantum indeterminacy' or even 'red shift', while a particle physicist would probably be equally baffled by the obfuscations of deconstructionism. But richness or poverty of vocabulary is usually deemed to be irrelevant to the issue of expressive power: the absence of 'myristicivorous' from one's vocabulary is not on a par with the absence of negation or coordination. Even the complete absence of number words beyond 'two', as Dixon (1980:107–8) reports for many languages of Australia, leaves the linguist's withers unwrung, especially when it is realized that the speakers of such languages have absolutely no difficulty in acquiring and using number systems as soon as they are exposed to them.

The colour terminologies of different languages are similarly disparate, with some having terms only for 'black' and 'white', others making no difference between 'green' and 'blue', and so on. This variation subsists despite the fact that there is no significant difference in the visual perception of humans around the world. Unless we are blind or have some visual defect – myopia, strabismus, nystagmus – we all see the same way and, except in cases of colour blindness, we all see colour the same way. On a conservative estimate, the average human can discriminate roughly half a million different colours (McGilvray 1994); about the same as the number of words in the *Oxford English Dictionary*. It follows trivially that we cannot have a word for each (detectable) colour, so it is perhaps unsurprising that different languages pick on different percepts to label.

Indeed, before the pioneering work of Berlin and Kay (1969) in the sixties, it was thought that languages divided the physical continuum of colours arbitrarily and without constraint. But their work claims to show a remarkable cross-linguistic commonalty. All languages have words for 'black' and 'white', and some languages have only those two. Some languages have three colour terms: words for 'black', 'white' and 'red', but no other colours. Next, some languages have four colour terms: words for 'black', 'white', 'red' and *either* 'yellow' *or* 'green'. Then some languages have five colour terms: words for 'black', 'white', 'red' and *both* 'yellow' *and* 'green'. Remarkably, *no* language seems to have three or more colour terms without having a word for 'red'; no language has five colour terms including 'blue' and 'brown' but excluding 'green' and 'yellow'. In brief, all languages appear to conform to the hierarchy:

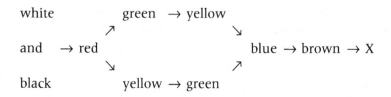

That is, if a language has *n* colour terms then those terms will correspond to the colours in the diagram, starting from the left and working in the direction of the arrows. No terms can be missed out, and it is only when you get to X, which stands for a range of possibilities such as 'pink', 'purple' and 'grey', that you get a free choice. Actually, the claim is a little more complicated than this. The first half-dozen terms must be 'basic'; that is, they should refer specifically to *colours* and not properties like 'sunburnt', which just have implications for colour. Moreover, they may be instantiated only once each: you can't have three words for 'yellow' before getting to a basic 'brown', for instance.

The immediate reaction of most people to this claim is that it's too good to be true, and must be wrong. In fact, evidence is still coming in, and the hypothesis is not secure, so it is worth looking at one or two cases which appear problematic. For instance, Chichewa (spoken in Malawi) has five basic colour terms, one of which (*chobiriwira*) translates 'blue' (Davies et al. 1995). This does not falsify Berlin and Kay's claim because *chobiriwira* translates 'green' as well as 'blue', and the native speakers' preferred identification of coloured chips to correspond to this term is in fact 'green'. Russian (see Corbett and Morgan 1988) is slightly less amenable: it has two words for 'blue' (*goluboj,* 'light blue', and *sinij,* 'dark blue') and no basic term for 'purple'. It is not entirely clear whether this falsifies the hypothesis or not, as there is disagreement as to precisely what constitutes a 'basic' term, and Russian does have an ('impure') word for 'purple' (*fioletovij*). Most difficult to accommodate is the colour system of the Ainu language of Japan, which is reported (Moss 1989) as having four basic colour terms, including one for 'red-green' (*hu*) and one for 'blue-yellow' (*siwnin*), which don't feature on the hierarchy at all.

However, if the hierarchy, or something close to it, expresses a correct generalization, it suggests a close connection between human cognition, perception and language. Further evidence for such a connection, evidence moreover which, like synaesthesia, seems to threaten notions of modularity, comes from the common psychological phenomenon known as the *Stroop effect*. Reading colour names is no problem: you've done it many times if you have got this far in the chapter. Even reading colour names when they are written in the 'wrong' colour is not significantly more difficult than reading them in the right colour. But naming the colour in which an incongruent colour word is written is both extremely disconcerting and quite difficult. Reading 'red' in normal print offers no problem; reading 'red' written in yellow, or 'green' written in blue, is mildly off-putting but not particularly hard; identifying that the word 'yellow' is printed in blue is dramatically harder, reflecting the fact that the written representation of the word 'interferes' with what it means.

It is interesting to consider whether this phenomenon constitutes a counter-example to Fodor's definitional claim that modular systems are informationally encapsulated: that is, that they are impervious to input from the 'central' system. The clearest example of such encapsulation is provided by the well known Mueller–Lyer illusion:

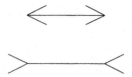

knowing (centrally) that the lines are the same length doesn't stop the (modular) visual system from *perceiving* them as different in length. But if our knowledge that 'red' means red interferes with our reading 'red' when it is written in blue, that looks suspiciously like the kind of cognitive penetration that informational encapsulation is supposed to exclude.

Fortunately, the vast literature on the Stroop effect includes experiments indicating that all is not lost for modularity. (For an excellent review, see MacLeod 1991.) Thus, not only is it harder to identify the (wrong) colours words are written in, it is harder to read *'bold'* printed in *italic* than in **bold**; more difficult to identify an 'H' made of 'a's than an 'H' made of 'h's; and so on.

```
h   h     a   a
h   h     a   a
h h h     a a a
h   h     a   a
h   h     a   a
```

In some Stroop variations, interference in identifying the colour can be exacerbated by semantic priming. For instance, if the task is to identify the colour in which the word 'nickel' is printed, then that task can be made harder by *priming* 'nickel' with a semantically related item, such as 'dime'. That is, identifying the colour that 'nickel' is written in takes longer than when it is not primed. Most importantly, such an increase is seen whether 'nickel' is primed by 'money' or by 'metal'. Given a sentence like *The toy cost a nickel*, where only the money interpretation of 'nickel' is relevant, interference is none the less also caused by priming with the word 'metal'.

The implication is that the interference occurs *after* retrieval of the word from memory. The central system is not infiltrating the module and causing interference (and violating Fodorian modularity); the interference emerges after the module has blindly served up the full range of possible interpretations – plausible and implausible – to the central system. The process is comparable to Swinney's elegant (1979) demonstration of what happens when you are confronted with sentences like *The spy hid the bug in the hotel room* and *The hygiene inspector found the bug in the kitchen.* He showed that, independent of context, *both* meanings of an ambiguous word like *bug* are initially accessed, and the irrelevant one is subsequently dismissed by the central system. The flow of information is *from* the input system *to* the central system, and never vice versa.

Exotic though they may seem, these phenomena of colour and language, from synaesthesia to Stroop, still fall under the generalizations of standard theories of the mind. Even if your perceptual wires are crossed, relations with and within the central system remain normal.

Note

This essay first appeared in 1996 in *GI* 2,6:9. I am grateful to David Pesetsky of MIT for correcting an error in the original version. Baron-Cohen and Harrison (1997) contains a number of papers on synaesthesia, and there is interesting recent work on the Stroop effect in MacLeod and MacDonald (2000). On the development of the number system, see Spelke and Tsivkin (2001).

6

The Structure of Noise

Humans are sensitive to sound along three different dimensions: language, music and noises. Language is complex, richly structured, largely innately determined – hence in large part universal – and subject to parametric variation. Music seems to share all these properties. Infants are universally sensitive to the perfect fifth (Gelman and Brenneman 1994); they have categorial perception of pitch and duration (Sloboda 1985); and there are systematic differences in the exploitation of the tonal continuum by different cultures – e.g. Indian and Western – that are reminiscent of parametric variation. Whether the choices among tonal and atonal, polyphonic and monophonic, or harmonic and aharmonic constitute parameters in the same sense as in linguistics is moot, but the overall effects of such choices are comparable, and distinct from the more idiosyncratic micro-parametric possibilities manifested by the throat singers of Tuva or the chanting of Tibetan monks.

Despite their common foundation on sound structure, mastery of music and mastery of language may, as a result of brain damage, doubly dissociate. After a stroke, the Russian composer Shebalin is reported (Sloboda 1985:260) as having had severe difficulties with understanding and reproducing speech, but as continuing to compose and to teach his students to the same high level as before; and the rare loss of musical ability can leave language intact.

What about the third strand? Are we innately predisposed to be sensitive to particular sounds? Do the noises we hear have complex internal structure in the same way as sounds of language do? Is there parametric variation for noise? I wish I knew. But it is gradually becoming possible to find evidence, mainly in the form of different pathological conditions manifest in auditory agnosia (see e.g. Polster and Rose 1998).

The richness of our auditory abilities is remarkable, although usually taken for granted – like most of our talents that are genetically determined. With your finger-nail, tap half a dozen different objects within reach: the table, the window, the chair, a book, a cup, your head – they all sound different. Think of the variety of birds and animals you can distinguish by ear; the auditory effect of walking into a familiar room from which the carpets or curtains have been unexpectedly removed; the difference between chinking coins and clinking keys. And consider that all these noises, despite being non-linguistic, connect to the relevant parts of your semantic memory, presumably accessing the same concepts as do words or images. (cf. Bregman 1990).

Such discriminations are independent of our linguistic (or musical) abilities. This was first brought vividly to my attention many years ago when I sat in on a demonstration of auditory agnosia by the neurologist Oliver Zangwill. He had a patient who, as the result of damage (probably) to the auditory cortex, was unable to understand spoken language, even though he was still able to read and was sensitive to noises. Showing that he was unable to understand spoken input was easy: his manifest distress at not understanding and the fact that he offered us a piece of paper to write things on were evidence enough. The next stage was most striking. After instructing him (in writing) to close his eyes, Zangwill proceeded to demonstrate that the patient could still differentiate the sound made by shaking a box of matches from that made by keys or coins or rubbing fabric. What was not so easy was to get him to open his eyes again: he couldn't understand what was said and, with his eyes shut, couldn't read . . . Gently touching his closed eyes solved the problem, but the dissociation between different auditory functions was remarkable.

Just as one can suffer selectively from aphasia or amusia, one can suffer from loss of the ability to discriminate 'environmental sounds' (as they are referred to in the literature), though diagnosis is rare, because the implications of such loss are dramatically less than those associated with losing one's language. Polster and Rose (1998) distinguish four types of hearing deficit: cortical deafness, auditory agnosia, pure-word deafness and phonagnosia. Cortical deafness affects the entire system, leaving victims unable to use their hearing in any domain. Although the next category is used inconsistently by different authors to refer to cases where language is or is not involved, 'auditory agnosia' can be characterized by the inability to recognize such sounds as coughing, whistling or a baby crying, while maintaining the ability to understand speech. In pure-word deafness, the patient may be able to identify the sex, age and regional origin of a speaker, while remaining completely incapable of understanding the utterances on the basis of which this information has been extracted. 'I can hear you talking but I can't translate it', as one person said (Polster and Rose 1998:54). Phonagnosia is a condition even rarer than any of the others, which is parallel to the kind of prosopagnosia which afflicted the subject of Sacks' *The Man Who Mistook His Wife for a Hat* (1985). In prosopagnosia, victims are unable to recognize a familiar face; in phonagnosia, they are unable to recognize a familiar voice.

Such cases indicate that we have precisely the kind of multiple dissociations in the auditory domain that we do in the visual and linguistic domains, and which provide prima facie evidence for modularity. The parallelism is not quite exact because the human brain is better constructed to withstand insult in the auditory domain than in the visual or linguistic domains. As mentioned in chapter 1, the right hemisphere of the brain largely controls the left side of the body, while the left hemisphere controls the right side. In fact, there are some connections from both hemispheres to both sides, and in the case of the auditory system there is greater richness of ipsilateral (as opposed to contralateral) innervation. Accordingly, it typically takes a bilateral lesion to give rise to auditory problems, whereas a unilateral lesion can sabotage sight or speech.

The existence of such dissociations (see also Franklin 1989) does not negate the fact that there are auditory abilities that appear to be common to the three domains. The most obvious example is our proficiency in locating the source of sounds with exquisite precision, whether these are musical, environmental or linguistic. We may not be as good at this as owls and bats, but we are pretty impressive. In fact, we can get some insight into the nature of our abilities by looking at other species a little more closely. It is famously the case that chinchillas share with humans categorial perception for Voice Onset Time (Kuhl and Miller 1975), suggesting that auditory categorization and discrimination are carried out in much the same way in both organisms, and maybe in mammals (or even vertebrates) more generally. Similarly, Suga (1995) has made interesting discoveries about moustached bats (and also barn owls), demonstrating that they have specialized areas of the auditory cortex which are excited only by sounds produced by conspecifics, and other – unspecialized – areas which are excited both by sounds from other bats (or owls) and also by sounds more generally. Presumably the closest analogues to conspecific sensitivity in humans are the language faculty on the one hand, and our instinctual reaction to a crying baby on the other.

What is still not clear is whether there are natural classes of (non-linguistic, non-musical) sounds. Are our sensitivities to noises parametrically selected in the same way as our linguistic and musical sensitivities are? It is clear that we have experientially induced differences. An expert ornithologist can tell apart bird-songs that are indistinguishable to the man or woman in the street, just as an expert cardiologist can tell a functional heart murmur from an organic one, and both from a normal heart beating. But are these differences 'categorial' in the way that contrasts in the perception of Voice Onset Time or the difference in detecting 'plucks' and 'bows' in music are; and are they selected on the basis of particular triggering data, as in language? I hope someone will write in and tell me.

It is one of the remarkable things about language that it is both universal and subject to (parametric) variation. Of what other domains can this be said? In general, there is no parametric variation (as far as we know) in purely sensory domains: humans around the world are essentially the same as regards their modular perceptual abilities. Where parametric variation occurs is in those quasi-modular (Tsimpli and Smith 1998) domains which are parasitic on sensory input but which, in virtue of incorporating bodies of domain-specific knowledge, are crucially part of the central system. Language provides the obvious example, but there are others: music and moral judgement, for instance. We have already seen putative parametric variation in music – the contrast between the twelve-note chromatic scale of Western music and the twenty-two-note *sruti* scale of Indian music, for instance. The incest taboo provides an example in the moral domain. All cultures have prohibitions on incest, constraining the set of people with whom you can enjoy sexual relations, but they parametrize them differently: some allow you to marry your cousin, other do not (van der Berghe 1983). Again, there is a problem deciding whether the notion of parameter is more than a linguistic metaphor in this case. At the very least, it seems unlikely that the triggering data are comparable, but that appearance may just be due to our ignorance.

Where does that leave us with noise? It would be interesting to know whether there are systematic differences in auditory discrimination in the domain of environmental sounds as there are in the discrimination of speech sounds and of music. There ought to be: even if urbanized Westerners have little hope of manifesting such contrasts, growing up in a jungle or by the sea, in the desert or on the tundra, should give rise to measurable alternations. To find out if that is true, we need some comparative auditory investigation of a wide range of populations. Looking for a PhD project?

Note

This essay first appeared in 1999 in *GI* 4,5:9. There is much more on this topic than I knew about when I first wrote it.

7

Dissociations

The poet Coleridge is reputed to have described the happiest possible marriage as 'the union of a deaf man to a blind woman'. While not exactly politically correct, this suggestion does highlight the kind of dissociation of the various faculties of man (and woman) which underlies much of current cognitive science: in particular, the Fodorian distinction between modular input systems and the central system(s). It is scarcely controversial that one can be blind without being deaf, or deaf without being blind, and hence that these senses are independent of each other. However trivial this might seem, it tells us something about how humans are organized: dissociation does not entail modularity, but it probably is the case that modularity entails (potential) dissociation. More interestingly, such relations provide a tool for looking at less transparent aspects of our make-up.

Consider first the incidence of haemophilia in the population. There are four logical possibilities: males with or without haemophilia, and females with or without haemophilia. In fact, only three of these combinations occur: although they can carry the disease, females virtually never suffer from it, so the category of 'female haemophiliac' is empty. There is only a single dissociation of sex and haemophilia, rather than the double dissociation of deafness and blindness. A similar example is provided by prosopagnosia and Capgras' Delusion. Prosopagnosia is the sad condition which afflicted Oliver Sacks' eponymous subject, 'the man who mistook his wife for a hat'. As a result of a cerebral lesion involving the visual system he became unable to recognize faces, even though he could still identify people from their voice or smell or touch, and his conceptual abilities were unaffected. In the even rarer case of Capgras' Delusion (e.g. Coltheart et al. 1997), faces are recognized perfectly, but this recognition evokes no emotional response and the identification of the person 'recognized' is therefore disbelieved by the central system. The sufferer may be convinced that the person whom he has recognized looks like his wife, but is simultaneously convinced that this person is an impostor, because there is no appropriate surge of affection (or antipathy). The outcome can be extreme, even resulting in the murder of the person who is deemed to be impersonating the one recognized. Again this is a case of single dissociation: prosopagnosia would make it impossible to suffer from Capgras' Delusion, because the preliminary recognition phase could never take place. There is none the less a potential conceptual distinction between this and the case of haemophilia in that, in principle, imaging techniques might show that afflicted individuals did indeed suffer from the lesions which cause both prosopagnosia and Capgras' Delusion, even though they could never give any behavioural evidence of it.

Dissociations of this kind have the appeal of the bizarre; they become relevant to the concerns of the (psycho-)linguist when one considers language and its interactions with other faculties, such as intelligence. There is a long tradition, best exemplified by the work of Piaget and his associates, which claims that the acquisition of language is crucially dependent on prior cognitive development. It is clear that language and intelligence can coexist (in you and me, for instance), or that both can be absent (as in anencephalic dwarves – those born with only a partial brain); and there are plausible cases where traumatic aphasia leaves people languageless but with their intelligence otherwise unimpaired (see, for instance, Sloboda's 1985 discussion of the composer Shebalin). What was supposed to be impossible was the possession of language in the absence of some degree of intelligence. Without further specification, the notion 'some degree' makes the issue hard to decide, but there is evidence from children with Williams syndrome that such views are simply wrong. Ursula Bellugi and her colleagues (Bellugi et al. 1993) have shown persuasively that these children have mastery of the syntactic constructions (passives, comparatives, and so on), whose acquisition is supposedly dependent on the achievement of the ability to pass seriation and conservation tasks, cognitive tasks that they consistently fail. In other words there is a double dissociation between language and intelligence, rather than a single dissociation.

Comparable double dissociations proliferate. The modular ability to recognize faces is clearly dissociable from language: Williams syndrome children are superb at both, but the polyglot savant Christopher (Smith and Tsimpli 1995), while wonderful at languages, is very poor at face recognition tasks, and Down syndrome children show the opposite distribution of abilities. Moreover, Christopher's problem with faces extends to a further dissociable domain: his short-term memory. His recognition of the faces of famous people, such as Margaret Thatcher or Saddam Hussein, is excellent, so his long-term memory in this area is on a par with his excellent memory for vocabulary. However, on standard short-term memory tests (e.g. Warrington 1984) he scores in the (high) normal range on the word section, but on faces he performs so poorly as to be off-scale.

Examples of this kind confirm that there is sub-modular dissociation as well as modular dissociation: the various parts of different modules can themselves be differentially impaired. Classic examples are provided by calendrical calculators, who, while often severely intellectually impaired, can tell you on what day of the week any date (past or future) falls. Such people typically have no other mathematical abilities, and little or no linguistic competence beyond the ability to respond accurately to such questions. As Stanislas Dehaene (1997) documents, there are many strange dissociations within 'the number sense', with the ability to make approximations ('about 20') and precise specifications ('exactly 7') being lost or preserved in different patients; and even the ability to add and subtract being differentially affected.

Similar dissociations occur within the language module. Christopher has a remarkable talent for learning morphological and lexical properties in a dazzling variety of languages, but his syntax in all of them (except his native English) rapidly reaches a plateau, so that his other languages are 'filtered' through English. In contrast, children suffering from spinal muscular atrophy seem to have a greater facility for inducing rules of syntax than for learning vocabulary (Sieratzki and Woll in press), and children with Specific Language Impairment have greater difficulty with inflectional morphology than with the rest of language (van der Lely 1997). The 'computational' part of the language faculty dissociates from the lexicon.

Dissociations of the kinds briefly (and simplistically) illustrated here are standardly used as evidence for modularity, with the tacit assumption that the results are valid not only for pathological populations but also for 'normal' people. Using such evidence in this way is justified only if people with brain damage are really like us: their brains are like ours, but have some component (or components) knocked out; they have not developed along fundamentally different lines, as though they were Martians. Logically, it might be the case, as Annette Karmiloff-Smith (1998) has suggested, that the mental make-up of such people is fundamentally different from that of the rest of us, so nothing about the modularity of mind in the normal population follows. The conclusion is unduly pessimistic. It is true that acquired and developmental disorders may need different interpretations, but there are no convincing cases where we have to assume that anomalous brain development leads to mental structures that are aberrant: these subjects are like us but with their talents and deficits thrown into stark relief by the asymmetries they manifest.

Dissociations provide evidence for modularity, but they also force us to rethink our notion of what modularity is – both because of such developmental considerations and because all the examples I've cited are really more complex than I've made out, and than used to be thought.

There are many examples, but one with interesting linguistic implications comes from research on memory by Daniel Schacter and his colleagues (1996). Subjects are notoriously unreliable at remembering which of a list of semantically related words they have really been exposed to. If you have heard *sharp, point, prick* and *pain,* you are likely to 'remember' hearing *needle,* even if you have not in fact heard *needle* at all. But your brain knows. Schacter used a PET scan to monitor the flow of blood in different regions of the brain while subjects were deciding whether or not they had heard the words before. This showed equivalent activity near the hippocampus (associated with memory) both for words that had been heard and for those that had not. But for those words that *had* been heard previously, there was additional activity in the left temporo-parietal region, an area responsible for processing auditory information.

So each input system fractionates into a number of independent sub-systems. We don't simply have (a set of) perceptual input systems feeding into a unitary central system, where the input modules are informationally encapsulated in Fodor's sense. Rather, there are different pathways for each input system, some of which are indeed encapsulated, but some of which are accessible to conscious introspection and – perhaps – manipulation. But this means that informational encapsulation, the major criterion for modularity, is more complex than has been generally credited. This is a two-edged observation: it allows modularity to be defended against a variety of attacks, but it makes refutation of the hypothesis much harder, because the precise claim of what modularity is becomes that much more complex and obscure.

Coleridge was not only politically incorrect, he was too simplistic by far.

Note

This essay first appeared in 1998 in *GI* 3,9/10:10. The literature on dissociations increases astronomically each year. For further references and discussion, see Smith (in press); Tager-Flusberg (1999). An interesting case of the maintenance of intelligence despite almost total loss of language is given in Varley and Siegal (2000).

Part II

Puzzles

8

Puzzle

Amahl was two and, like all very young children, had difficulty pronouncing the words he was learning. *Duck* came out as 'guck', *knife* became 'mipe', and his *Magic Roundabout* hero was consistently mangled into 'Gougal'. As a linguist I was intrigued to work out why my son made these 'mistakes'. Did he have difficulty hearing? Did he need speech therapy? Or were these pronunciations just examples of normal development and open to rational explanation?

The first task was to discover whether he could hear the differences between the sounds in the adult language. He pronounced many words identically, saying 'mout' for both *mouth* and *mouse*, for instance. Seeing how hard the French find it to separate such pairs, it seemed likely that he just couldn't hear the difference. However, when I put pictures of a mouth and a mouse in a different room and asked him to 'bring me the picture of the *mouse*' or 'bring me the picture of the *mouth*', he always fetched the right one.

So that hypothesis was wrong. At least he could hear well enough, and clearly knew more than his performance indicated. His linguistic 'competence', as the jargon puts it, was only imperfectly reflected in his speech.

So maybe the reason for his mispronunciation was simply that, like the French, he was unable to get his tongue round some English sounds. This guess turned out to be inadequate too. There were certainly some sounds he had not learnt to pronounce, but there were some puzzling exceptions. As well as changing *Dougal* into 'Gougal', Amahl consistently pronounced *bottle* as 'bockle', *pedal* as 'pegal' and *puddle* as 'puggle'.

This was interesting because the change was so regular that his behaviour was clearly rule-governed, not random: knowing that he pronounced *zoo* as 'doo' and *lazy* as 'lady', for instance, changing the adult 'z' into 'd', enabled me to predict that he should pronounce *puzzle* as 'puddle'. As indeed he did. But if he pronounced *puzzle* as 'puddle' then the reason for pronouncing *puddle* as 'puggle' clearly could not be that he was simply unable to say 'puddle'.

And there were other bafflements. I had noticed that he pronounced the 'n' in *hand*, but left out the 'm' in *jump*, even though 'm' and 'n' are as close to each other in pronunciation as they are in the alphabet. I asked him to say 'jump'; he responded with 'dup'. I asked him again; again he said 'dup'. Finally, I said, 'No, say "jummmmmp"', and he replied 'Only Daddy can say "dup".' What did he think he was saying when he told me only I could say 'dup'?

Moreover, if I presented him with his own pronunciations – either imitated or tape-recorded – he interpreted them as though they were mine. At three, when he was pronouncing both *mouth* and *mouse* as 'mouse', we had the following exchange:

Me	What does 'mouse' mean?
Amahl	Like a cat.
Me	Yes, what else?
Amahl	Nothing else.
Me	It's part of you.
Amahl	(*Disbelief*)
Me	It's part of your head.
Amahl	(*Fascinated*)
Me	(Touching his mouth) What's this?
Amahl	Mouse.

Only a few seconds later did it dawn on him that they were the same.

To explain all this we need a theory of the child's linguistic mind. The simplest model would be that in which adult pronunciations are changed into infantile ones by a single set of rules. That is, the adult pronunciation and the child's mental representation are equivalent, and this representation is converted by a set of rules to give the child's pronunciation. The rules vary from child to child, but within strict limits. For instance, Amahl's versions of *duck* and *Dougal* are examples of 'consonant harmony'. Thus the 'd' in *duck* and *Dougal* is pronounced in a different part of the mouth to the 'ck' and 'g' later in the same words (try saying them slowly); but the velar 'g' Amahl used instead of the alveolar 'd' is pronounced in the same part of the mouth. The 'd' harmonizes to 'g' to make things easier. Consonant harmony is common, and the full range of possibilities – what kind of rules can feature, in this first model – is largely predicted by linguistic theory. For instance, Amahl's cousin, Robin, also showed the effects of this consonant harmony: even though he pronounced *duck* 'correctly' as 'duck', he pronounced *fork* as 'gork'. He had the same universal process but instantiated on a different class of sounds.

Unfortunately, this simplest model does not work. Although Amahl could tell *puddle* and *puzzle* apart, and even pronounced them differently, there were some adult contrasts between which he simply could not discriminate: *puddle* and *puggle*, for example.

Of course, there is no adult word *puggle*, so it was hard to tell this at first, but mistakes he made with other words, such as pronouncing *pickle* as 'pittle', changing 'ck' to 't' rather than vice versa, showed that he had (temporary) perceptual problems. It was enough, however, to necessitate a change from the first model to a second model, in which perception is accorded an explicit place. In this model, adult pronunciation goes through a perceptual filter to give the child's mental representation, and it is this representation which is then converted by a slightly smaller set of rules to give the child's pronunciation.

We can now explain most of Amahl's behaviour. He said 'puggle' for *puddle* and 'pittle' for *pickle* as a result of perceptual difficulty. He said 'guck' for *duck* and 'mout' for both *mouth* and *mouse*, not for any perceptual reason, but as a result of general (universal) tendencies which apply in slightly different ways to any child learning any language.

Finally, to explain what he was thinking when he said 'Only Daddy can say "dup"', we need to assume that, despite his pronunciation, he could keep the adult pronunciation for *jump* in mind. As this was the same as his mental representation, it is not surprising. What is surprising is that 2-year-olds are so complex and so interesting.

Note

I have been preoccupied with this puzzle for nearly thirty years. I first discussed it in Smith (1973:55) and have revisited it periodically ever since: e.g. in my 1989 ch. 4 ('The puzzle puzzle'). The insight about Amahl's perceptual difficulty is due to Macken (1980); the model informally sketched here appears in Smith (1978), which post-dated Macken's paper. A version of the current essay appeared in the *Independent* on 23 April 1990, under the title 'A child's crossed words puddle'.

9

PC

When I first started reading scholarly articles on linguistics as a student, I was fascinated to see that their distinguished authors obviously communicated with each other by postcard. It was only some time later that I realized that 'p.c.' stood for 'personal communication'. Later still, I came across personal computers, privy councillors, police constables, and prescriptions enjoining me to take my pills *post cibum*. Life was filling up with potentially confusing abbreviations. But the latest is more serious. I have been attacked by political correctness.

I had been long familiar with the exhortations of those who told me that I should avoid sexist or racist language, and I was sympathetic to their cause. However, I was also unwilling to perpetrate sentences like *The reader may easily persuade herself that muffins are addictive* unless I knew that the reader was female; or *The reader may easily persuade themself that muffins are addictive* unless I believed 'them' to be schizophrenic. For me, *himself* felt gender neutral, but accepting that my grammar was offensive to some, I tried bravely to strike a happy compromise by writing *him or herself* instead.

I am prepared to go that far in the interest of verbal hygiene (the title of an interesting and perceptive book by Deborah Cameron), and I enjoy some of the convoluted jokes ridiculing those who suggest more extreme examples: like 'actuarially mature' for *dead*, or 'intra-species dining' for *cannibalism*. But my latest exposure to politically correct language convinces me that things have gone too far.

A few years ago I wrote a book called *The Twitter Machine* (1989), (some of) which is being translated into Farsi, the language of Iran. The author of the translation wrote me a courteous note explaining that certain of my examples 'raised problems', and asked if I would be prepared to supply alternatives illustrating the same points. The first example was a triplet of sentences exemplifying the tenses of English, as in (1):

1a. The prime minister resign*ed*
 b. The people *are* happy
 c. There *will* be dancing in the streets.

I could understand that the mullahs of Qom might not be too happy with this sequence of putative events, and suggested that *died* instead of *resigned*, and *sad* in place of *happy*, might be acceptable. In fact, it turned out that what was in danger of giving offence was not what I imagined, but the mention of dancing. Other examples that seemed to be in need of censorship are listed in (2):

2a. Fred was seduced by a mermaid
 b. Esme kissed me
 c. She loves me

I find it slightly sad that (2a) should arouse such puritanical anathema; sad, but understandable. What I find nearly incomprehensible and deeply depressing is that there should be a culture in which just writing a sentence like *She loves me* is deemed to be unacceptable, subversive, or politically incorrect in any way. It's sad, but is it significant? Is political correctness in language a serious issue that linguists should concern themselves with?

I must admit that for a time I was dismissive and treated the whole thing as a rather weak joke with irritating overtones. The irritation sprang from the need to modify my style along the lines indicated and also a grudging suspicion that maybe the campaigners had a point. Linguists, of all people, should be sensitive to the nuances, and the power, of language, and I was somewhat taken aback on two counts: I had been failing to notice some of the more subtle propaganda underlying certain usages, and I had been unaware of the complexity of the issues involved.

Cameron (1995:136) cites an example I already knew: George Bush's defence of the invasion of Panama with the words 'We cannot tolerate attacks on the wife of an American citizen.' I had seen it before for a piece of chauvinistic rabble-rousing. I had not noticed that it was also sexist, with its covert implication that 'American citizens' were male. Reading such examples and pondering the thought processes which must have prompted my Farsi translator to write to me gave further food for thought.

Most people try to be polite and courteous, or at least try not to be gratuitously rude, so only the most unreconstructed bigot would refer to someone as a 'queer nigger' rather than a gay black, or whatever designation seems contextually appropriate (where this will clearly depend on one's own colour, sexual preference and a host of other factors). The desirability of elementary politeness is sufficient reason to modify one's language. Some stigmatized usage may seem trivial or irrelevant to you, but this 'triviality', allied with the fact that it is important to others, makes it incumbent on you to change your ways if you can.

Other examples are not a matter of politeness, but have more sinister implications. When a government spokesperson argues that a particular course of action will result in the loss of 'jobs' for the workers, it is as well to scrutinise the context carefully and see if what is really at risk are 'profits' for the mandarins (see e.g. Chomsky 1993b:68). Similarly, 'moderate' regimes seem always to be those which are friendly to us; 'peace-keeping' is whatever we do – whether it involves real peace or armed aggression is irrelevant (Chomsky 1983:171, 188). Such Orwellian usage can be insidious, as it is both similar to and crucially distinct from the case of sexist language. The difference is that there is no issue of politeness or personal sensibilities involved, so superficially there might appear to be no issue. The similarity, which generalizes to the Farsi case I began with, is that the usage reflects the preconceptions of the dominant group and is aimed, consciously or unconsciously, at preserving a culture which will reinforce the status quo. The status quo may be one of white male domination, of capitalist domination, or of religious domination. In every case the resources of language are recruited to bolster the power base of the elite.

This diagnosis is relatively simple; what to do is not always obvious. Politeness is no threat to our liberties, though it is worth remembering that activism may be necessary to make us realize that we are not being polite. Misrepresentation of the truth and outright censorship – the respective techniques of the liberal and the totalitarian – need to be opposed. At least, that much is clear if – like me – you believe that no censorship is defensible. But if you share that belief, you have a duty and a problem. If you believe in the right of people to say whatever they like, however evil or sexist or racist it may be, because the alternative of censorship is worse, that brings with it the responsibility to speak out against the unspeakable – to make sure that the arguments of the bigots are refuted and that you do not lose the freedom to say what *you* wish as well. That is the duty; the problem is what to do in the case of those whose (freely expressed) views may include inciting the mob to murder you for yours.

There is a conflict of incompatible fundamentals: the absolute right of the individual to exercise freedom of speech versus absolute obedience to higher authority, whether sacred, as in the case of Islam, or secular, as in the case of fascism. In both cases, a crucial realization is that language is normative, and some norms are transcendentally better than others, so we must argue for them (see Nagel 1997). Ultimately, the only hope is that rationality will prevail; assuming, of course, that one's own position is rational.

Many aspects of the campaign for political correctness in language have the stamp of authoritarianism, but the campaign is harmless if it stops short of censorship, and is beneficial if it brings to conscious awareness the perennial need for challenge to all forms of authority. Strictures against sexist language challenge (typically) the authority of male dominance; strictures against racist language challenge (typically) the authority of white supremacy. Whatever the power structure, you can guarantee that it will arrogate to itself the right to exercise linguistic hegemony as it does economic or military hegemony, deriding the dissidents as it does so. Awareness of this hidden agenda is prerequisite to opposing it. Ed Herman's (1992:164) definition of 'politically correct' as 'The challenge of dissidents and minorities to traditionally biased usages and curricula, as perceived by the vested interests in existing usage and curricula' is precisely right. I must send him a postcard.

Note

This essay first appeared in 1998 in *GI* 3,3:8.

10

Acquired Whining

According to Woody Allen 'sentence structure is innate but whining is acquired' (Sunshine 1993:190). The first proposition will be reasonably familiar to most linguists, but I imagine that the second is less expected and, in part for that reason, mildly amusing. So what makes Woody funny? What makes *anyone* funny come to that? The literature on humour is notoriously unfunny, but a little theoretical insight is breaking into even this murky area, so it's worth trying to see how some of it works.

Everyone agrees that incongruity is a crucial element in most forms of humour, where incongruity ultimately reduces to contradiction. This raises two problems: first, there is nothing funny in asserting the contradiction that 'All swans are white and not all swans are white'; second, it is not immediately obvious how examples like 'acquired whining' contrive to be contradictory at all. These problems suggest that the contradiction has to creep up on you unawares: it has to be *implicit* rather than *explicit*; and it has to be something you are led to construct indirectly for yourself: it is not straightforward and it cannot work without your involuntary collaboration.

In recent work exploiting Relevance Theory (Sperber and Wilson 1995), Carmen Curcó (Curcó Cobos 1997, 2000) has spelt out some of the issues involved in making these intuitive assumptions precise. Her first point is that the most important notion is not the incongruity itself but the effects achieved by processing incongruity. Indeed, she makes a strong case for the claim that the analysis of humour requires no special theoretical apparatus which is not independently needed for the analysis of normal communication. Processing utterances is an inferential activity, carried out in conformity with the communicative principle of relevance, which gives you a guarantee that what is being said is going to have cognitive effects without putting you to gratuitous effort. In order to achieve such effects you are often constrained to provide an appropriate context on your own responsibility. If you ask whether *Husbands and Wives* is worth seeing, and are told 'all Woody Allen's films are great', you are forced to supply the implicated premise that the film is by Allen, because that is the only way the answer can be construed as relevant.

Consider in this context the following excerpt from a policy document put out by the Ministry of Transport in Dublin shortly after Ireland had joined the European Union:

> For a two-year experimental period, beginning at midnight on 31st December, cars will drive on the *right* (as in the rest of Europe), instead of the *left* (as in the UK). If the experiment is a success, buses and lorries will thereafter also drive on the right.

As you read, you naturally interpret 'cars' as a generic term for vehicle, because this is the only rational meaning in a context where rules of the road are concerned and hence will be mutually manifest to speaker and hearer. That is, you construct a scenario including the tacit assumption 'All vehicles will drive on the right.' When you get to the punch-line, you are forced to supply an implicated premise to the effect that 'cars' excludes other types of vehicle, hence that 'Not all vehicles will drive on the right.' The writer has deliberately not made this explicit but, by trading on the presumption that processing the utterance will be relevant, he gives you no option but to access this new, contradictory, premise: he has lured you into making incongruous, contradictory, assumptions. The point of the analysis is not to show *why* the particular example is funny, but (if it is funny) *how* the effect is, in part, achieved.

Incongruity is usually disguised, and the nature of the disguise can be revealed using another construct from relevance. Part of the interpretative process involves treating something which should be in the foreground as though it were in the background. Another example from Woody Allen can be used to make the point:

> There is no question that there is an unseen world. The problem is how far is it from midtown and how late is it open? (Sunshine 1993:255; cited in Curcó Cobos 1997:214)

As you process an utterance, you make anticipatory hypotheses about what is coming next (Sperber and Wilson 1986:202ff; for discussion, see Smith 1989:ch. 14, 'In my language we shout'). Whether a hypothesis is in the *foreground* depends on a variety of factors, including the syntactic structure of the sentence being uttered, the order in which the constituents are introduced and, crucially, whether it is relevant in its own right. What is in the *background* is information that can be taken for granted. With the current example, it is obvious that the subject pertains to the supernatural, which, by hypothesis, refers to a domain which is not located in space and time the way the physical world is. Accordingly, when you have got as far as 'The problem is . . .' you expect to hear next a putative solution to a 'problem' about the supernatural. What you get is an answer which presupposes something of incontestable relevance: it would overturn all our conceptions of the occult if it were true, but it is something which is presented as though it were just part of common background knowledge: that the unseen world is physically located near midtown.

It is presented this way, but it is equally clear that the proposition being put forward is not really being endorsed by the speaker. Another crucial strand in the manipulation of humorous effects depends on the notions of dissociation and metarepresentation. Intuitively Woody Allen is distancing himself from the claim that the unseen world is accessible from midtown, and is indulging in a degree of (self-)mockery in the way he describes it. This dissociation is in turn dependent on the possibility of using a representation not just to *describe* a state of affairs, but to *interpret* (or metarepresent) another representation. The classic case of such 'interpretive use' is found in irony. If I say 'I do admire the president's honesty', it is likely to be clear that I am intending to ridicule anyone defending the proposition that the president is honest (even if no one actually has), and that I am simultaneously dissociating myself from such a proposition, perhaps with contempt.

Dan Sperber (1994a) has emphasized the surprising complexity of metarepresentation in everyday conversation, arguing that speakers and hearers regularly entertain at least fourth-order metarepresentations. If John says to Mary that there is an unseen world, then:

John intends
– Mary to know
– that John intends
– Mary to believe
– that John believes
– that there is an unseen world.

Assuming that Mary is not so credulous, she will construct a representation of the kind:

John says – there is an unseen world, but I believe – there is not an unseen world – So John is mistaken.

If Mary believes that John doesn't really believe there is an unseen world, she will construct the more complex representation:

John says – there is an unseen world, but I believe – that John believes – that there is not an unseen world – So John is lying.

It is a further step or two on the same progression before we get to the situation where the conclusion is that John is joking or being ironic:

Mary believes – that John believes – that Mary believes – that John believes – that there is not an unseen world – So John may be joking (or demented).

If Curcó Cobos is right to claim that to get a humorous interpretation a contradictory proposition must be embedded in a metarepresentation of at least the fourth order, it is not surprising that some people consistently miss the point of jokes and witticisms. Indeed, some people, specifically autists, are congenitally incapable of understanding jokes. Autists are customarily characterized as lacking a 'Theory of Mind', so they cannot impute beliefs to others: alternatively, they cannot metarepresent, so jokes are in principle beyond them. Ianthi Tsimpli and I described one such person in chapters 3 and 4 above, but most of us are familiar with the situation in which we cannot really tell whether someone is joking or not.

It is clear that the quotation from Woody Allen that I started with was inspired by his admiration for Chomsky (see, for instance, 'The Whore of Mensa' in Allen 1975). It is intriguing that the respect is mutual, and Chomsky has been known to cite Woody Allen in his most serious work. For example, in *Rules and Representations* (Chomsky 1980:117) he refers to the fact that ' "The universe is constantly expanding" . . . the discovery that turned Woody Allen into a neurotic.' I leave it to the reader to work out the correct depth of metarepresentational embedding that an appropriate understanding of this remark requires.

Note

This essay first appeared in 1998 in *GI* 3,5:9. The literature on humour is vast. For a savage review, see *Index on Censorship* 29, 6 (November/December 2000), especially Rowson (2000). For recent work on autism, see Happé (1999).

11

Godshit

In *The War of Don Emmanuel's Nether Parts* a particularly obscure passage in a termite-eroded philosophy book is described as being like surrealist verse or the product of 'an American disciple of Wittgenstein' (de Bernières 1990:28). The combination of familiarity, erudition and slight condescension makes this a striking image: the more striking the more one knows about both Wittgenstein and American academics. 'Images provide / a kind of sustenance' (Raine 1979:20) and they have sustained workers in the language industries for generations, even if the traditional 'myth of mental imagery' – that we think in images rather than words – has long been out of favour among philosophers and psychologists. Imagery is now largely the domain of literary critics, with the role of linguistics, at least of current theoretical linguistics, being marginal or even non-existent.

In a perceptive analysis of imagery Tannen (1989) discusses the effects of authenticity, involvement, intimacy and aesthetic pleasure that can be derived from images in conversational discourse, and hints that the current linguistic paradigm has no room for them. This position is understandable if one limits the scope of the paradigm to syntax and phonology, but not if one casts the net a little wider. A complete account of the language faculty clearly necessitates a pragmatic theory of utterance interpretation, even though this involves central processes that go beyond the modular properties of the language organ in Chomsky's sense. Given an appropriate allocation of duties to different components of the language faculty, I want to argue on the one hand that imagery succumbs in general to analysis in terms of one particular pragmatic theory – Sperber and Wilson's (1995) Relevance Theory – and on the other that it provides a useful test for certain claims of that theory.

The heart of Relevance Theory is the two-fold claim that the relevance of an assumption can be assessed in terms of contextual effects and processing effort: the greater the effects, and the smaller the effort needed to achieve them, the greater the relevance. Contextual effects are typically a synthesis of the old and the new: they constitute information which the hearer could deduce neither from the utterance alone nor from the context alone, but only from the combination of both. For instance, the utterance in (1):

1. That painting is by Keating

is relevant in the context given in (2):

2. If that painting is by Keating, it is a worthless forgery

because it implies the conclusion in (3):

3. That painting is a worthless forgery

which is deducible neither from (1) alone nor from (2) alone. (See Smith 1989:74.)

The need to minimize processing effort means that it is normally more relevant to tell your questioner (truthfully) that 'the station is straight ahead' than to tell her or him (again truthfully) that 'the station is straight ahead, assuming that you are referring to the nearest station'. The second is unhelpfully prolix, forcing the hearer to process unnecessary material.

It is frequently the case that an image can be more cost-effective than a straightforward, purely factual description. That is, literal truth may be less important than the evocation of a wide range of weak implicatures: assumptions that have been triggered by the speaker but for which the hearer has to take some responsibility. This responsibility derives from the fact that the context of interpretation for any utterance is always in part idiosyncratic to the hearer, as her or his encyclopaedic knowledge is necessarily different from that of the speaker. In the case of de Bernière's American disciple of Wittgenstein, the implicatures drawn by the reader are only in part predictable by the writer. Some, perhaps many, readers of this book will have more knowledge of Americans and Wittgenstein than either de Bernières or me; all will have different knowledge, leading to different evoked stereotypes of academics or of the choice of extracts from the *Tractatus* to compare to surrealist verse.

Does this mean that truth and truthfulness are irrelevant to utterance interpretation? Wilson (1995) has argued persuasively that a (Gricean) maxim of truthfulness is unnecessary provided one has a notion of resemblance sufficient to characterize the shared implications which it is the speaker's intention to convey to the hearer. Even though it is strictly false that (American disciples of) Wittgenstein produce prose which is reminiscent of surreal verse, the similarities are sufficient to license the image: both are confusing, wilfully obscure, unrewarding, and so on.

The question of truth is not so clear-cut. In the postface to their book, Sperber and Wilson have attempted to deal with the fact that, in general, only *true* information is worth having, and hence relevant, by modifying their definition of relevance to refer to *positive* cognitive effects: those which lead to *true* beliefs. In partial motivation of the change, they provide (1995:264) a beautiful pair of examples, reproduced in (4):

4a. Peter is a jealous husband. He overhears Mary say on the phone to someone, 'See you tomorrow at the usual place.' Peter guesses rightly that she is speaking to a man, and infers, quite wrongly, that she has a lover and does not love him any more.

4b. Peter is a jealous husband. He overhears Mary say on the phone to someone, 'See you tomorrow at the usual place.' Peter guesses wrongly that she is speaking to a man, and infers, rightly as it happens, that she has a lover and does not love him any more. (Mary's lover is a woman.)

As the same assumption may, in different contexts, be either true or false, and as true assumptions may give rise to false beliefs and vice versa, it follows that an assumption may be relevant or not largely irrespective of the richness of the beliefs it gives rise to. This leads Sperber and Wilson to say that a particular proposition may *seem* relevant when in fact it is not. This is unfortunate. Knowledge, as opposed to belief, is a metaphysical category, not a psychological one. Whether a particular proposition is true or false is often unknowable, and if in some cases its truth value becomes known, this is frequently irrelevant to its fruitfulness in human cognition and communication. It seems to me that their earlier definition of relevance without the 'positive' is still preferable.

Consider in this regard the extract in (5) from the *Totecuyoane*, a sixteenth-century Nahuatl address to the Franciscan missionaries, cited by Brotherston (1992:140):

5. They gave also
the inner manliness, kingly valor
and the acquisition of the hunt:
the insignia of the lip, the knotting of the mantle,
the loincloth, the mantle itself;
Flower and aromatic leaf, jade,
quetzal plumes, and the godshit you call gold.

'Godshit' is a wonderful image for gold. It endows it with positive and desirable supernatural attributes, yet it indirectly ridicules European attitudes towards it, putting them in a perspective at once sardonic and superior. As with any image or metaphor, my interpretation may differ in various ways from yours and, crucially, there need be no truth claim implicit in the description. As a twentieth-century European I suspect that gold is *not* godshit. I might even go so far as to say that I know it isn't. Whether the Aztecs believed it was I don't know. It probably comes in that class of apparently irrational beliefs that characterize all cultures, and which Sperber (1985, 1994b) describes so felicitously in terms of 'reflective' belief and metarepresentation.

Suppose that someone believes or believed that the image is literally true, just as some people believe in the literal truth of many propositions in the scriptures of various religions. Any appeal to an 'increase in knowledge' (Sperber and Wilson 1995:266), where knowledge is defined in terms of truth, is going to alter the relevance of the propositions including it.

This again seems undesirable. The contextual and cognitive effects of the image are independent both of its truth and, more importantly, of the truth of the propositions one entertains as a result of processing it. For me 'godshit' successfully suggests that Europeans were stupidly preoccupied with something simultaneously base and noble; for someone else the collocation in the image may be simply blasphemous. In both cases the cognitive effects are great, independently of the truth of these suggested propositions.

Imagery is too important to be left to the literati. As our understanding of the use of language gradually catches up with our understanding of knowledge of language, we can use pragmatic theory to illuminate the study of imagery while simultaneously using imagery to refine the theory. Relevance Theory sheds interesting light on all the tropes; that light is brighter when truth is left aside.

Note

This essay first appeared in 1996 in *GI* 2,5:10. Deirdre Wilson assures me that the argument is wrong. In particular, she points out that Sperber and Wilson were making a metaphysical not a psychological claim, and the psychological implications of their theory remain unchanged by the change in the definition of relevance. The ultimate motivation for this modification is then evolutionary: 'the evolutionary goal is genuine knowledge' (D. Wilson, p.c.). I confess to remaining sceptical about the notion of 'evolutionary goal', but I am relieved that the psychology can stay as it was.

Recent (psychological) work on imagery can be found in Kosslyn (1994); Richardson (1999).

12

The Golem

Linguists like to think of themselves as scientists, constructing impressive theoretical edifices, making falsifiable predictions, revising their hypotheses on the basis of crucial findings, always striving towards the truth: all the things that real scientists do in explaining their bit of the universe. But then we risk getting tarred with the brush that is used to paint a less attractive picture of the scientific community, constructing self-serving pseudo-explanations, rigging the data, revising the theory to vacuity: all the other things that real scientists do in defending their share of the cake.

In a pair of insightful and inspirational books, Harry Collins and Trevor Pinch (1993, 1997) have likened the scientific enterprise to the workings of the Golem, a creature of Jewish mythology who is part supernatural slave, part evil genius; driven by truth, but unaware of either its own power or its own ignorance. This amalgam of contradictory properties provides a revealing metaphor for science, and can help explain why it is sometimes seen as unmitigated evil, sometimes as a peerless knight in shining armour. In fact the literary treatment of the Golem does not altogether gibe with Collins and Pinch's account. Meyrink's (1928) and Singer's (1983) eponymous novels, for example, show the Golem either as an ill-omened and intangible threat, or as a kind of cross between the Sorcerer's Apprentice and a *deus ex machina*. But the metaphor is revealing.

Collins and Pinch elaborate two complementary stories: first, the discoveries of scientific endeavour are never as pure and clear-cut as they are (regularly) made out to be, and hence, second, there is room for the social interpretation and manipulation of those findings, just as much as there is in less rigorous domains. Even paradigm examples of crucial experiments turn out on inspection to have been not quite so straightforward: Einstein's theory of relativity won final acceptance when there was apparent corroboration of its prediction about the bending of light in the 1919 solar eclipse. But the positive interpretation of the observed results was due to the machinations and the imaginations of influential establishment figures, in just the same way as the interpretation of political decisions is often a function of power structures and not simply the 'truth'. Moreover, there was ample contradictory evidence available that was simply ignored, and younger scientists had anyway accepted the truth of the theory beforehand, because it made sense of the world as nothing else did. The 'crucial' experiment was wonderful for propaganda, less important for the real practitioners. This revisionary version of the events should not be taken as detracting from the fact that Einstein's prediction, and the theory from which it derived, reflected real genius and progress: no one any longer accepts the *pre*-Einsteinian world view even if, *post*-Einstein, relativistic explanations are giving way to newer and yet more exotic ones. It also bears noting that Einstein's work is widely viewed (again not entirely justly or straightforwardly) as having paved the way for the horrors of the nuclear age, from Hiroshima to Tokaimura, or wherever the latest 'unpredictable' accident occurs.

While not in the same league when it comes to underpinning disasters, the situation in linguistics is not dissimilar. Consider the 'linguistics wars', a phrase used as the title of a book (Harris 1993) and to characterize the perceived conflict between 'generative semanticists' and 'interpretivists' in the 1960s. Whatever the merits of this particular account, the perception that the combatants were indulging in internecine hostilities is widely shared. It is equally clear with hindsight that the knock-down arguments of the antagonists should have been less decisive than (perhaps) they were. Much of the argumentation revolved around the role (if any) of the technical device of transformations within generative grammar. Much of the initial success of transformations had been due to the fact that they solved descriptive problems, almost as miraculously as the Golem solved the problems of persecuted Jews. And even when explanatory issues, such as learnability, were raised, other phenomena – unbounded dependencies, for instance – were adduced as incontrovertible evidence of the need for transformations. But as was subsequently shown, there are innumerable *descriptive* devices that can be made to do the same work – slash categories of the kind introduced by Gerald Gazdar (1980), for instance – so the arguments were not as powerful as one might wish. The debate continues forty years on: recent work confronting derivational and representational systems (e.g. Brody 1997, 2000; Chomsky 2000b) shows that evidence purporting to demonstrate the need for transformations is empirically extremely difficult to pin down. Comparable remarks pertain to empty categories – in part another off-shoot of transformations – which have been interpreted as powerful evidence for the innateness of aspects of the language faculty. In many corners of the field the existence, and this interpretation, of empty categories is uncontroversial orthodoxy; in other corners, of course, linguists have no truck with empty categories. The possibility of falsification is moot.

Such tensions and different perceptions are characteristic of the core of the discipline. The situation is similar, indeed starker, when we move to the differing viewpoints of theoretical and applied linguistics, or look from outside the discipline entirely. Consider the latter first. Linguistics (and linguists) can certainly polarize opinion. On one account, 'linguistics . . . is or are the scientific study of language – never, perhaps a tremendously useful discipline at the best of times, but reduced by Chomsky and his disciples to a positively mind-boggling level of stupidity and insignificance' (cited in Smith 1989:1). On another account, Chomsky was reputedly described by the philosopher Richard Montague as one of the 'two great frauds of twentieth century science' (cited in Smith 1999:4); the other was Einstein, so at least he was in good company. For most readers, as for me, I suspect that the perception of Chomsky and his work is rather different, even if not all of you would put him up (again) for the Nobel prize. But what is relevant here is that we have demonization alternating with beatification, with the same characters appearing as the embodiment of either good or evil.

It is not difficult to dismiss both the attacks and the adulation as the result of ignorance compounded by insecurity. But, as Bob Borsley and Richard Ingham (in press) have recently argued, we should perhaps take note when people describing themselves as linguists seem equally intemperate. The focus of their attention is a series of claims, implicit or explicit, from 'applied linguists', arguing that it is radically misguided to concentrate on knowledge of language rather than the use of language, or that the whole enterprise of theoretical linguistics should be replaced by the study of texts. Some of the claims they discuss miss their mark in that they pertain not to linguistics but to the sociology of ideas, but if it were true that there is no valid study of language 'without a social dimension', then much of the work of 'theoretical linguists' would be worthless. We hope we have achievements to gainsay such claims, but this institutionalization of incomprehension is none the less worrying; and though it may again result from ignorance tinged with insecurity, we should perhaps be prepared to combat it.

A more telling complaint is the converse of the above, and one where we are the guilty parties: theoretical linguists often proclaim their discipline as the only valid, scientific approach to language, forgetting that the reach of science is not very far. We are all pressured by the need for funding to try to make our work seem relevant and 'applied' to those who hold the purse-strings: many grant applications end with a pious appeal to the (putative) fact that the research for which funding is being solicited will have radical implications for anything from man–machine interaction to teaching in primary schools. We need to admit with greater openness that the ambit of linguistics is extremely limited: the Golem cannot see very far. Other, non-scientific, disciplines may have greater insight into some areas of language study than we do.

Even so, as emphasized in the opening chapter, linguistics does have a certain amount to say about the 'applied' domains, from TEFL to speech therapy, from the law to archaeology. It is not for nothing that teachers, as well as speech and language therapists, receive a training in phonetics and linguistics, even if it is still largely a mystery *how* rehabilitation, for instance, works (Robertson 1999). Even English literature might be illuminated by some of the insights emanating from the work of linguists: consider, for instance, the work on metrics described by Nigel Fabb (in press) or on poetic effects within Relevance Theory (see e.g. Wilson and Smith 1992).

But in general, even though we may be able to cast light on them, we don't *solve* the problems of other disciplines, and we shouldn't pretend that we can. Given the universality of feelings of insecurity, it is easy enough to tread Golem-like on the toes of our specialist colleagues; it is even easier to tread on the toes of those in different departments. But we live in an age of interdisciplinarity, and if we are going to benefit from the insights made in other areas, we must tread on more toes – and expect to have our own trodden on in return. Scientific unification of the findings from different disciplines may be still over the horizon, but a certain integration of understanding may be possible somewhat sooner.

Unification and integration both presuppose that we can transcend personal preoccupations; as Chomsky puts it (1991:3): 'to the extent that a subject is significant and worth pursuing, it is not personalized'. A Golem is not quite a person, but we can use the analogy of science as a Golem to reinforce both this and another point: the ambivalent nature of the scientific enterprise underlines why naïve falsificationism (the view that you give up your theory if it makes any false predictions; see Lakatos 1970) is not good enough. Our theories must indeed engender hypotheses which are falsifiable *in principle*, but the tests that we devise for the theory will rarely give clear-cut results, as the Golem can always provide an auxiliary hypothesis to save the theory. Alternatively, and confusingly, he can also provide a radically different, perhaps non-scientific, perspective on the problem being addressed. But non-science is not nonsense; so we need tolerance as well as rigour; and there the Golem can help.

Note

This essay first appeared in 2000 in *GI* 4,9/10:6. The Golem is currently in hiding.

13

$

Student: What is an operator?

Me: An operator is a function whose output is of the same kind as its input.

Student: That's too abstract. Give me some examples and tell me how many operators there are.

Me: Well, there are Negative operators, WH operators, Tense operators, Modal operators (of Necessity and Possibility), Relative operators, sundry Quantifiers (Universal, Existential, Degree, Generic, and maybe a few more), Comparative operators – when should I stop?

Student: But how many *types* of operator are there?

Me: Well, there are one-place operators, like INFL, *not* and *who*; and two-place operators like *because* and *which*. There are binding operators, like WH, *every*, *who* and *which*; and non-binding operators like *not*. There are empty or null operators, of the kind found in infinitival relatives and purpose clauses; and overt operators, like *very* and various WH words and phrases. There are subordinating operators, like *although*; and coordinating ones, like *and* . . . I could go on for a long time.

Student: But . . .

Me: Yes, and *but* is one too.

Student: Start with something easy.

Me: We'll begin with one-place versus two-place operators, go on to binding and non-binding operators, and continue with subordination and coordination, first separately, then simultaneously. For instance, minor and functional category heads can be either one-place operators like *very* and *must*, giving rise to examples such as: *Penguins look cute, Penguins look very cute, Penguins must look cute*; or two-place operators like *so* and *because*, yielding examples like *Because penguins look cute, I am addicted to them* or *He insulted my penguin, so I hit him*.

Student: OK – that's easy enough.

Me: The next difference is that between binding operators like WH, which bind a trace in examples like *Which penguin did you see t?* and operators like *not* which don't bind anything in examples like *Penguins are not edible*. The two types cross-classify: a determiner like *every* is a two-place binding operator, so *Every penguin looks cute* is analysed such that *every* first binds the theta-role of *penguin* to project a noun phrase, and this in turn binds the theta-role from *looks cute* to give the appropriate VP. However, some determiners, such as *no*, can be either one-place, as in *Mary considers no penguin employable*, where *no penguin* is an argument; or two-place, as in *Mary considers her penguin no fool*, where *no fool* is a predicate (Cormack 1995a:242).

Student: This is becoming excessive. Couldn't we get rid of some of these operators (and penguins)? For instance, we already have too many empty categories, and null operators have been viewed with suspicion, or even categorically outlawed, by quite respectable people (e.g. by Steedman 1997:6).

Me: Yes, but provided you have good evidence for them even empty operators are defensible, and may even have phonological effects. For instance, the (empty) yes/no Question operator can bring about intonational differences of the kind seen in *He is coming?* (as opposed to *He is coming!*). Moreover, Santelmann (1999:286f) argues elegantly that null operators have great explanatory potential in first-language acquisition, so empty operators are as well motivated as any of the others.

Student: All right, I'll grant you those.

Me: Thanks. In fact, I think there's good evidence for the claim that we need *more* operators. In particular, Annabel

Cormack (with a little help from her friends; see the references beginning with 'Cormack') has argued persuasively for a new kind of – generally null – operator that she calls $, pronounced 'dollar'. I should hasten to add that the name is not due to any capitalist proclivities, but was chosen as it is available on a computer keyboard and is usefully reminiscent of '&'.

Student: OK, tell me about this $.

Me: Everyone is familiar with subordination and coordination and their different syntactic properties. For instance, *for* and *because* are near synonyms but contrast sharply in behaviour. While both the examples in (1) are acceptable, even if (1b) is a little mannered, the contrast between the corresponding pair in (2) is very sharp:

1a. I'm leaving, because he makes me nervous
 b. I'm leaving, for he makes me nervous

2a. It was because I was nervous that I left
 b. *It was for I was nervous that I left

This difference has traditionally (e.g. Smith and Wilson 1979:39) been attributed to the fact that *because* is a subordinator and *for* is a coordinator, and coordinate structures are relatively resistant to manipulation. Moreover, it has often been taken for granted that subordination and coordination are mutually exclusive and exhaust the space of possibilities. But this is only true if you ignore the fact that coordination is only one kind of conjunction. Anyway, building on traditional accounts of 'subordinating conjunction', and working on the assumption that all structure is head mediated (Cormack and Breheny 1994), Cormack has argued for a new operator head, $. Furthermore, she suggests that once we've got this new operator, it can be used to replace modifying adjunction, and it can also play a crucial role in accounting for and unifying a large number of superficially disparate phenomena.

Student: Hold on, just give me an example of what $ actually does.

Me: All right, consider a domain where the coexistence of subordination and conjunction can be seen clearly, namely in serial verb constructions (Cormack and Smith 1994) and their near equivalents in English: so-called 'quasi-serials' like (3):

3.   John ran and fetched a frog.

Semantically, this clearly involves conjunction: both running and frog-fetching must crucially be involved if the sentence is to be true. Syntactically, things are not so clear. In superficially comparable examples like the coordinate structure illustrated in (4):

4.   John yawned and extinguished the light

it is impossible to extract the object, hence the unacceptability of (5a):

5a.   *What did John yawn and extinguish?

But the apparently parallel (5b) is impeccable – a fact which has puzzled syntacticians since Ross (1967) introduced the coordinate structure constraint:

5b.   What did John run and fetch?

The reason for the asymmetry seen in (5) is due to the fact that (4) involves genuine (coordinating) conjunction, usually symbolized by '&', whereas (3) involves subordinating conjunction, symbolized by '$'. That is, we have an operator – $ – that combines aspects of both subordination and conjunction, which (assuming that the Ross constraints or their equivalents apply only to genuine coordinating conjunction) gives us exactly the right results.

Student: Hmm. Now that we have a $, what else can we buy with it?

Me: A representative selection of wares is provided by the examples in (6):

6a. The red frog
  b. No boy riding a bike
  c. Mary left the room angry
  d. Susan ate the meat raw
  e. Pablo painted the girl naked
  f. Jake painted the barn red
  g. They drank themselves silly

Intersective adjectives as in (6a) are nicely accounted for, as their semantics (RED & FROG) is that of generalized conjunction (Gazdar 1980), but the adjective is syntactically subordinate to the noun. Similarly, post-nominal modifiers like *riding a bike* in (6b) are combined with their head by the mediation of $; depictives, both subject-oriented and object-oriented, of the sort seen in (6c) and (6d) respectively (or ambiguously in (6e)), and resultatives as found in (6f) or (6g), all succumb naturally to the power of dollar. If you're sceptical, read the references, beginning with 'Cormack'.

Student: Is that it? Can it do anything else?

Me: A further use for $ can be seen in adjectival complementation, where there is also evidence that, like other heads, it constitutes a landing-site for movement. In examples like *red frog* or *fat penguin*, we have the simplified structure in (7):

7. [$ fat [penguin]]

but with *A penguin fatter than yours* the penguin has climbed up the tree into $ as in (8):

8. [$ fatter than yours [penguin]]
    ↑_____|

Student: Neat. Is $ universal?

Me: It's part of UG, but it's subject to parametric variation. It's a head, so in some languages it occurs initially (as in

English), in others it occurs finally (as in Nupe – see Cormack and Smith 1994). It may have different selectional properties – selecting verbs as opposed to adjectives, or VP as opposed to TP, for instance (see Cormack and Smith 1999); and in some languages and constructions it may be overt, while in others it is usually covert.

Student: So it's not always empty after all – examples please.

Me: We've already seen one. It is overt in English quasi-serials such as (3) above. That is, in English the lexical item *and* may realize either coordinating & or subordinating $, and $ itself may be either overt, as in (3), or covert, as in (6). Another overt example is provided by Tadzhik (Nichols 1986:58). In this language, there is a suffix (-*i*) which marks the syntactic dependency between the constituents in examples like *red frog*: a dependency which is not expressed overtly in English. I take it that this is another visible instance of $.

Student: So $ is a universal, asymmetric, subordinating, two-place, non-binding operator, which may be overt or covert? I need a drink.

Note

This essay first appeared in 2000 in *GI* 4,7:7. Annabel Cormack and I are still working on exploiting $ as much as possible.

I am grateful to Annabel Cormack for holding my hand while I wrote this column, saving me from making several egregious errors. She is not to be held responsible for the remaining ones, which I have left in as a challenge to the reader.

Part III

Polemics

14

Bonobos

Bonobos are clever. One bonobo in particular, called Kanzi, seems to be very clever indeed. He can respond to simple sentences of spoken English, obeying (sometimes disobeying) a wide variety of commands; he can produce appropriate responses to questions by using sequences of lexigrams – colourful abstract symbols arranged on a computer keyboard; and he has learnt to do most of this without being explicitly trained but, like any young child, simply by being immersed in a linguistic environment. It would appear that Kanzi in some sense has the faculty of language and, as he can indulge in pretend play, he may also be endowed with a 'Theory of Mind'. In a passionately argued book (Savage-Rumbaugh et al. 1998), Sue Savage-Rumbaugh, Stuart Shanker and Talbot Taylor make both these claims, and contend further that 'the linguistic competencies displayed by Kanzi . . . potentially undermine the assumptions that undergird much of modern linguistics, psychology and philosophy' (1998:181). More forcefully still, they come to the conclusion that 'current explanations regarding the manner in which our species acquires and passes on language have to be incorrect – not just partly, but completely incorrect' (1998:206).

As the 'current explanations' that they impugn include those provided by generative linguistics, it seems desirable to look a little more closely. Several issues arise. First, are the factual claims about the linguistic abilities of Kanzi and other bonobos (*Pan paniscus*, a relative of the chimpanzee) justified? Second, if they are, do they really have such dire implications for linguistics and associated disciplines? Third, is the putative truth of these claims about bonobos and other apes prerequisite to adopting an appropriate moral relationship to them?

It is clear that Kanzi can communicate with human interlocutors, at least in part through the medium of English. The extent to which this communication exploits the kind of grammar standardly attributed to humans is less clear, and the authors seem surprisingly, and explicitly, reluctant to find out. For instance, in a section headed 'syntax grasped' (1998: 65) they document Kanzi's reaction to 660 different English sentences, noting that he responded correctly to 72 per cent of utterances of the kind exemplified by 'Put the tomatoes in the melon' or 'Knife the doggie' (*sic*). By contrast, a $2\frac{1}{2}$-year-old child presented with the same sentences was deemed to have responded correctly only 66 per cent of the time. Unfortunately, the criteria for a 'correct response' are not spelt out, and some scepticism is prompted by the remark that Kanzi's reaction to 'Put some water on the carrot' (namely to throw the carrot outdoors) was accepted as correct, because 'it was raining very heavily at that moment, and tossing the carrot out into the rain was certainly a satisfactory means of getting it wet' (1998:69). There *are* pairs of sentences such as 'Pour the Coke in the lemonade' and 'Pour the lemonade in the Coke', but we are not told how these were reacted to. More importantly, there are no details of any attempts to devise tests which would necessitate either ape or child using grammatical knowledge, rather than simply having recourse to a large vocabulary and a modicum of common sense about what you can do with, say, a knife and a doggie once you have identified both. Still less are there any tests of the statistical significance of responses on such tests. This is surprising and disappointing, as Kanzi obviously does have a large vocabulary, a considerable intelligence, and a willingness to interact with humans, so testing would be easy.

Further, when it comes to the details of syntax, the text is inconsistent in its claims about Kanzi's ability. On the one hand, it is freely conceded that he doesn't have the expertise of (adult) human speakers; on the other, it is repeatedly claimed that he does 'have language'. A generous interpretation of the examples which are provided suggests that Kanzi has at most an ability comparable to that of a child at the prefunctional level of language acquisition. If this were correct, it would put him on a par with the average 2-year-old, and account for the inconsistency that both display with regard to word-order and the encoding of grammatical relations, for instance. It would still be inappropriate to describe him as being at a 'pre-functional *stage*', as there is no evidence that he will ever progress to the next (functional) stage, and not even evidence that his system, however lexically sophisticated it may be, obeys the principles of UG (such as structure dependence) characteristic of all stages of language acquisition in children.

But there are deeper problems. Much of the philosophical discussion in the book presupposes a Wittgensteinian theory which implicitly denies any distinction between language and use of language (1998:136). Moreover, the concept of 'language' used is not the I-language of current (generative) linguistics, but a rather crude, behaviourist version of E-language (1998:208). 'Language is a funny thing. We do not think of it as behavior, yet at heart that is all it really is' (1998:226). It is clear that the existence of a shared public language, independent of the human mind, and of which individuals may have partial knowledge, is necessary for their position that Kanzi 'has language' in anything like the same sense as we do. Unfortunately, it is therefore also clear why it is unnecessary for the average linguist or psychologist to lose any sleep over their conclusions.

Consider what the aims of linguistics and psychology are. I take it that the goal of both disciplines is to devise theories which will enable us to understand and explain human competencies. For the last quarter of a century the most successful steps in this enterprise have been made by modular theories of cognition, which ascribe to humans, *qua* humans, a language faculty, a moral faculty, and a variety of other domain-specific abilities, which are in large part innately determined. Interesting evidence for such theories comes from dissociation: language may be dissociated from intelligence or from Theory of Mind; one part of language, such as the syntax, may be dissociated from another, such as the lexicon, and so on. (See chapter 7 above.) What is important about this modular paradigm in the current context is that it represents a position radically different from the one Savage-Rumbaugh and her colleagues are attacking, and is in fact immune from any such attack.

Providing necessary and sufficient conditions for what constitutes 'possessing a language faculty', as though 'language' existed independent of its users, is at best a pseudo-issue, at worst incoherent; and much of the authors' discussion of what might constitute such conditions results in nothing more than erudite obfuscation. I imagine that their response would be that my formulation of the domain of linguistics is already 'speciesist', but this would be either simplistic or disingenuous. Much of contemporary linguistics has striven to show that the notion of language they are presupposing is just not an appropriate domain for theory construction (e.g. Chomsky 1995a). Humans, octopuses, bonobos and chairs all have arms, but we don't have a theory about creatures with arms that encompasses all of these. Chinchillas (and probably bonobos) have categorial perception of voicing contrasts, just like human neonates; so there is another domain in which we are not unique. This may be fascinating, but it doesn't follow that we should, or even could, devise a theory of all those things which share this property. Science isn't like that.

There are other places where the object of the authors' attacks is misconceived. They seem to think that communication is an exclusively coded, rather than a largely inferential, procedure (1998:101), and that linguists neglect the fact that it is necessary to study language in context (e.g. 1998:195). It is accordingly rather sad that there is no reference to any of the work in pragmatics that attempts to devise a cognitive theory of communication, based on an explicit account of context. They are similarly misinformed about current views on first-language acquisition in humans, attacking in particular the 'Chomskyan' position. But as they assume that this involves the child in 'seeking, testing, hypothesizing' (1998: 91), it is not one that Chomsky or anyone working in a principles and parameters framework would recognize. They likewise ignore much of the work in Theory of Mind, a term they use frequently, but only occasionally with the implications familiar from work in cognitive psychology. Presumably this is because while pretence is within Kanzi's ability, the imputation of false belief is not. Most strikingly, there is no reference to a Fodorian language of thought (Fodor 1975).

I take it that Kanzi has a language of thought, but that it is not as rich as that of humans. It enables him to carry out elementary inferencing to solve some problems, but his language of thought is not systematically related to a natural language, as it is in humans. He may have a vocabulary comparable to that of a 2-year-old, but evidence for *any* natural language syntax is lacking or anecdotal. Kanzi is (perhaps) quite good at exploiting his talents for the purpose of non-verbal communication, but it is simply false that this can 'serve just as well to express or communicate what one is thinking' (1998:135) as language. There is an overlap in what can be communicated, but it is perverse – or dishonest – to deny a difference because of that overlap. The claim that he has a mastery of 'formalism' commensurate with that of human language and that this leads to the conclusion that our notion of language is incorrect – in particular, that we have 'to abandon the view that such formalisms are innate in man or ape' (1998:194) – is simply a fallacy: the antecedent is false and the conclusion a non sequitur.

The authors have demonstrated that bonobos have considerable intelligence, and that they can interact interestingly with humans. Should we rethink our morality, our concept of the nature of humanity and our understanding of linguistics, psychology and philosophy as a result? I see no reason to think so. Take the issue of morality and 'speciesism'. I am happy to agree that we should treat bonobos, dolphins, whales (and especially frogs) with consideration, compassion and kindness (though I draw the line at being nice to the anopheles mosquito). But this attitude does not depend on a demonstration that any of them share my linguistic ability to understand spoken English. Kanzi is fascinating, but none of the radical claims made on the basis of his abilities is justified.

Note

This essay first appeared in 1999 in *GI* 4,3:9. See now Povinelli (2000), who claims that chimps fail to understand elementary notions of causation that are transparent to toddlers. For contrary views, see Dunbar and Barrett (2000), Tomasello and Call (1997) and Hauser (2000). There is ongoing disagreement about how *intelligent* chimps are; there is little serious work claiming that their linguistic abilities are remotely comparable to those of small children.

15

Whales, Sunflowers and the Evolution of Language

Chomsky is fond of describing linguistics as a branch of psychology, ultimately biology. This places the study of language firmly in the area of the natural sciences, grouping it with genetics and chemistry, rather than poetics or literary criticism, and inviting evaluation of its theories by the standard scientific criteria of simplicity, elegance and truth. In his recent book *Biolinguistics*, Lyle Jenkins (2000) provides a reasoned defence of this position, and a sustained attack on those who have misrepresented various aspects of the generative enterprise.

The core problems of (bio)linguistics are, first, to define what constitutes knowledge of language; second, to determine how that knowledge is acquired; third, to find out how it is put to use; fourth, to uncover what the brain mechanisms underlying it are; and finally, to investigate how it evolved in the species. Other essays in this book devote considerable space to each of these five domains, but it is the question of evolution which has recently elicited most (and mostly uncomprehending) attention, which attracts the largest part of Jenkins' fervour, and on which I will concentrate here.

The background is Chomsky's (1995b) 'minimalist-internalist' view of language. It is minimalist because it eschews any constructs which are not conceptually inevitable or forced by empirical necessity (so no more deep structure, for instance); it is internalist because the notion of 'language' that supports any coherent theorizing is as an internal construct of the individual mind. This construct is largely innately determined: we are born knowing the principles of grammar, and the huge variety of the world's languages results from the setting of a number of 'switches' or parameters, on the basis of triggering data from the environment. The claim of innateness, perhaps the most controversial implication of Chomsky's programme, is motivated *inter alia* by universal properties of language and by the fact that all, and only, human infants learn the language they are surrounded by, and do so on the basis of a rather impoverished input. Universality does not force one to conclude that aspects of language are innate, but in the absence of plausible alternative accounts, innateness is overwhelmingly the most likely explanation.

If knowledge of language is largely innate and common to the species, then it is presumably genetically determined. If it is genetically determined, but our relatives – from chimpanzees to mushrooms – have no comparable language faculty, then it must have evolved. But now there is a problem, as Chomsky is widely quoted, most particularly by Dennett (1995) and Pinker (1994), as denying that natural selection could have produced human language. Furthermore, as there are supposed to be only two possible explanations for evolution, namely 'God or natural selection', Chomsky must either be appealing to divine providence or be a mystic. Jenkins documents the details of the debate at considerable length, and establishes beyond reasonable doubt that this crass characterization of Chomsky's views is radically, perhaps maliciously, misguided.

Chomsky's position is *not* that natural selection has played no role in the evolution of language, but that natural selection is only one of many factors. In all evolution, whether of language, the eye or an antibody, an essential contribution is also made by physical and developmental factors working on the variation provided by random mutation. Consider whales and sunflowers.

Whales are big; so big that they would not be viable on dry land. As has been known since Galileo (see Thompson 1942:30), there are different growth constraints on skeletal form for aquatic animals, because buoyancy diminishes the effect of gravity. It is uncontroversial that natural selection played a role in the emergence of 150-ton mammals but, equally uncontroversially, this selection took place under a variety of physical constraints. This is most obvious when one compares whales with terrestrial animals: the advantages of size are largely the same on land and water, and are equally likely to be selected for, but growth on dry land is subject to limitations which are irrelevant in the ocean. In other words, the evolutionary growth of whales is not just a function of natural selection.

Sunflowers show a different facet of the complexity of evolution. Sunflowers have two interlaced families of spirals in the head, one going clockwise, one anti-clockwise. The numbers of florets in each spiral are typically adjacent terms in a Fibonacci series (the series obtained by starting with 0,1 and summing the previous two terms to get the next: 0, 1, 1, 2, 3, 5, 8, 13, 21, 34, ...). It is implausible that the genes determine that the flower produce 21 seeds in one direction and 34 in another, rather than 22 or 36, for instance: that's not the sort of thing genes do. In fact it is now known that this mathematically fascinating property of sunflowers and other organisms arises as a result of the timing of the emergence of the primordia during development. Again, the emergence of a particular property is not due solely to processes of natural selection.

How is this relevant to the evolution of language? The standard criticisms of Chomsky with regard to evolution are based on a simplistic, and sometimes dishonest, analysis of the range of possibilities available, and of Chomsky's position on them. His realistic evaluation that evolution is extremely complicated and that we know next to nothing about it is represented as a denial of *any* role for natural selection, despite frequent assertions to the contrary. This travesty often comes with the suggestion that refusing natural selection an exclusive role is equivalent to mysticism. Jenkins demonstrates in meticulous detail both what the real state of affairs is, and what Chomsky's admittedly speculative contribution is. Properties of language have evolved. Natural selection must have played a role in this evolution, but so too have elementary physical constraints, such as the size of the human head. Many other factors have also, presumably, been involved, such as the adoption of a trait in one domain for use in another: an example might be the exploitation of discrete infinity by both the number sense and the language faculty. That is, just as there is no highest number, there is no longest sentence, so the set of numbers and the set of sentences are both infinite. Further, the two infinite domains are both 'discrete'. What this means is that sentences are always constructed out of a whole number of words (the preceding sentence contains exactly twenty-one words, not twenty-one and a half), just as large number such as 83,472 can be constructed by adding exactly one to the preceding item (83,471). In fact, both 'number' and 'language' can exploit non-discrete infinities as well: you can always insert some fraction between two adjacent numbers (21.5 between 21 and 22; 21.25 between 21 and 21.5, and so on); and in language you can speak more loudly or softly, faster or slower, in a continuous, non-discrete fashion. We share such non-discrete infinities with other organisms in the animal kingdom; discrete infinities are much rarer, perhaps unique to us. Our knowledge of any of the details of evolution are vanishingly small, but the questions are coherent, the issues are empirical, and the problem of unifying the various bits of our knowledge with the rest of the natural sciences is standard.

Since Jenkins finished his book, Chomsky has returned to what he calls an 'evolutionary fable' (2000b:94), emphasizing that 'little is known about evolution of higher mental faculties, and it is not clear how much can be learned within the limits of contemporary understanding' (2000b:141). The core of his story is initially rather disappointing: 'Suppose some event reorganizes the brain in such a way as, in effect, to insert [the language faculty]' (2000b:94). But as Martin and Uriagereka (2000:12ff) point out, even this fable has a number of properties which set it apart from the standard views of writers like Pinker (1994) and Plotkin (1998). First, the standard neo-Darwinian view is gradualist, whereas Chomsky's fable posits a sudden event: the evidence is meagre and hard to interpret, but the rapid emergence of art, of tool use and of a complex social life are not incompatible with the abrupt appearance of language. Second, Chomsky's view is modular, assuming that the language faculty is an autonomous system interacting with the rest of the mind/brain, whereas Pinker's is constructivist, assuming no principled distinction between decoding and inference (see Origgi and Sperber 2000 for discussion). Again, the evidence is not totally transparent, but various versions of the modularity hypothesis have had considerably more success over the last twenty-five or so years than their constructivist rivals (see e.g. Chomsky 1975; Fodor 1983; and innumerable others). Third, neo-Darwinian explanations typically appeal to such processes as the gradual favouring of unambiguous constructions (e.g. Pinker and Bloom 1990), ignoring the fact that ambiguity and underdetermination are rife in language, and that linguistic processes frequently give rise to ambiguity. For instance, ellipsis of the sort which produces *John loves Mary more than Susan* from the more complex *John loves Mary more than Susan does* simultaneously makes it indistinguishable from the reduced form of *John loves Mary more than he loves Susan*. None of these points is decisive and, as has already been stressed, the major valid observation in this domain is that we are ignorant. But as Martin and Uriagereka (2000:15) put it: 'Chomsky's evolutionary fable is, at worst, better than its competitors and, at best, even somewhat plausible.'

Note

A version of this essay appeared with the title 'Truth in the silence of mushrooms?' in the *Times Higher Education Supplement* (9 February 2001) as a review of Jenkins (2000). The study of the evolution of language is blossoming. Recent books include Carruthers and Chamberlain (2000), Cavalli-Sforza (2000), Knight et al. (2000), and many others. A sane set of suggestions for what might gradually have emerged is provided by Jackendoff (1999). The evolution of speech (as distinct from the evolution of language) is discussed in Fitch (2000). On 'constructivism' more generally, see Quartz (1999).

16

Jackdaws, Sex and Language Acquisition

It is well known that when goslings hatch they 'imprint' on the first moving thing they see and follow it around devotedly. Usually the first moving thing they see is a mother goose, so the process is evolutionarily advantageous on the assumption that identifying Mum is a good survival strategy. Goslings are not the only creatures who use this technique. In his classic treatise on ethology, Konrad Lorenz (1970) tells the sad story of some jackdaws that he and his colleagues had raised from eggs, and which accordingly imprinted on them, presumably in the mistaken belief that they were mother birds. In fact, ethologists make pretty good mothers compared to the average jackdaw, and all went well for the fledglings until they reached sexual maturity. At this stage they tried (unsuccessfully) to mate with their surrogate conspecifics, with pathetically frustrated results. Interestingly, they did not try to mate with the individual scientist on whom they had initially imprinted, but made sexual overtures to any other human that they came into contact with. It seems that these jackdaws had distinct mental representation for humans in general, and for their specific human 'parent' in particular. Even confused jackdaws avoid incest. A second interesting observation, and one which will finally make this esoteric excursion into the sex life of *Corvus monedula* not totally irrelevant to those expecting to read something about language, is that this imprinting has to take place within a very narrow critical period soon after hatching. Just like first-language acquisition.

At a colloquium recently one of my colleagues said that he was under the impression that no one believed in a critical period for language acquisition any more; that the idea had gone the way of alchemy or phlogiston, or deep structure. I hastened to disabuse him: not only is there a critical period for language acquisition but, as Lynn Eubank and Kevin Gregg (forthcoming) have argued, there are probably several critical periods for language acquisition.

Though their discrimination of different humans suggests that some aspects of their behaviour must be due to the environment, it is clear that the imprinting of goslings and jackdaws is genetically determined: there's just no time for the responses to be learned. Genetic determination comports well with the existence of critical periods, so if our language faculty is (partly) innate, we should expect to find a critical period for first-language acquisition. Genetic determination does not entail the existence of a critical period or periods, so there is no necessary connection in that direction, but if a critical period does exist it would be highly suggestive of innateness. So what is the evidence – in humans, that is, as opposed to jackdaws?

There are at least eight different kinds of evidence and, on the assumption that explanatory convergence is important, I intend to mention all of them.

First, there is evidence from normal first-versus second-language acquisition. It is uncontroversial that everyone acquires a first language reasonably painlessly, but that learning another one after childhood is only rarely so successful. All linguists know that MIT linguist Ken Hale's 'ultimate attainment' in numerous 'second' languages is amazing, but it's precisely because it is amazing that he doesn't constitute a counter-example to the general claim. For normal people, first-language acquisition has to take place within the window of opportunity that constitutes the critical period, or they are doomed to sounding like foreigners for ever.

Second, there is evidence from (differential recovery from) aphasia. In a classic book, which first spelt out the plausibility of postulating a critical period for language acquisition, Eric Lenneberg (1967) argued that there was an inverse relationship between age at injury and degree of recovery from acquired aphasia, so that the older the child, the less good the outcome, with complete recovery seldom being achieved for lesions acquired after puberty. As might be expected, there are putative counter-examples to this position, the most striking being the development of language in a 9-year-old boy after hemidecortication (the surgical removal of half the cortex of the brain to inhibit epileptic seizures; see Vargha-Khadem et al. 1997), but the general claim has been maintained over thirty years.

Third, there is evidence from 'wolf children' like Genie, the girl who was kept locked up in an attic in Los Angeles from the age of 2 to 13, and was exposed to virtually no language until her release. Sue Curtiss anticipated that Genie would provide a refutation of the critical period hypothesis and claimed that 'in the most fundamental and critical respects, Genie has language' (Curtiss 1977:204). But although Genie did indeed master an impressive vocabulary, with all sorts of subtle distinctions of colour, shape and texture, her syntax crucially appeared to remain minimal. There has been controversy as to whether Genie's traumatic childhood, or even pre-existing mental damage, invalidates using her case in evidence, but as we know of many children with worse cognitive deficits who none the less acquire a near normal syntax, it seems defensible to use her both as support for a critical period for the acquisition of some aspects of syntax and against the idea that there is a critical period for learning vocabulary. (See also Bloom and Markson 1998.)

Fourth, there is evidence from Down syndrome. Language acquisition in Down syndrome is generally delayed, but there is considerable individual variation in speed of development and in ultimate attainment: some subjects never achieve proper mastery of language, others approximate normality. Crucially, if this development extends beyond puberty, normal language is never achieved, and those rare subjects with apparently normal language (Rondal 1995) have achieved it before then. If correct, this scenario constitutes further evidence for a critical period ending around puberty.

Fifth, there is evidence from the acquisition of Sign Language by the deaf. In an elegant study, Rachel Mayberry (1993) compared various groups of long-term users of American Sign Language: those who had learnt ASL as a first language in infancy; those who had learnt it as a first language in later life, having been brought up essentially without language; and those who had learnt it as a second language after having gone deaf. Her results demonstrated that 'late-second'-language learners significantly outperformed the 'late-first'-language learners, suggesting that acquisition of language early in life is necessary for language processing to be carried out efficiently in later adulthood, with the implication that there is a critical period for the normal acquisition of the first language, which is prerequisite to successful second-language acquisition.

Sixth, there is evidence from the language of the deaf–blind. Those who are born doubly disadvantaged in this way never acquire a normal first language; those who, like Helen Keller, go deaf–blind after the age of about 18 months may (given suitable coaching) achieve normal command of language through the medium of touch. Such examples and the case of Tadoma that I wrote about earlier (chapter 2) not only show the necessity of postulating a critical period, but indicate that it must be operative in the first months of life.

Seventh, there is evidence from imaging experiments using fMRI and PET scans. Kim and colleagues have demonstrated that second languages appear to be stored in different places in the brain depending on the age at which they were acquired: 'within the frontal-lobe language-sensitive regions (Broca's area), second languages acquired in adulthood . . . are spatially separated from native languages. However, when acquired during the early language acquisition stage of development . . . native and second languages tend to be represented in common frontal cortical areas' (Kim et al. 1997:171). If there is a critical period for language acquisition, this dissociation would be (partially) explained, as would the difference in mastery of first and second languages referred to above. Eighth, there is evidence from the case of Christopher, the savant whom Ianthi Tsimpli and I have observed over the last ten years (Smith and Tsimpli 1995). One of Christopher's more striking properties is a dissociation between his morpholexical ability and his syntax. He appears to be able to learn new vocabulary items and complex morphology without limit, but the syntax of his twenty 'second' languages is filtered through English. If there is a critical period for the setting of parameters, and if these are associated with functional categories, we have an explanation for this asymmetry.

Ninth . . . but maybe that is enough, except to say a little bit more about the plural in critical period*s*. It is a commonplace that a foreign accent can persist in the presence of perfect syntax, and it seems clear that there are different critical periods for the two domains. Indeed, Peter Jusczyk's (1997) work indicates that there may well be separate critical periods for different parts of phonology: the perceptual properties of the vowel system seem to be fixed before those of the consonant system, for instance. But this should be enough to convince even my sceptical colleague, and simultaneously to show that we have plenty to learn from the birds.

Note

This essay first appeared in 1998 in *GI* 3,7:7, but the critical period hypothesis is still controversial. The results on bilingualism are similarly contested; a recent discussion is given in Hernandez et al. (2000). There is interesting discussion of the genetic basis of various cognitive disorders in humans in Isles and Wilkinson (2000).

17

Does Chomsky Exist?

Let me reassure those of a nervous disposition that the answer we shall arrive at is, probably 'yes'. As most people reading this will never have doubted the fact, it may seem curious that I pose the question at all, especially as there is a common myth (1994b:170) that there are two Noam Chomskys: the political activist and the linguist. I have even interviewed prospective students for a linguistics degree who expressed mild disbelief when I assured them that the author of *Deterring Democracy* and *Year 501* had made a not insignificant contribution to the subject they were blithely preparing to devote the next three years of their lives to.

The question is prompted by puzzles about the relation between words and things, between thoughts and states of affairs. The accepted wisdom is that our utterances reflect our beliefs, our beliefs are made true or false by facts that exist independently of us, and hence we may perhaps not be the ultimate authority on what our own words mean. The conclusion is discomfiting.

In his discussion of reference, Chomsky is wont to make remarks about 'there being no external reality' (1993a:43), to say that 'The question, "to what does the word X refer?", has no clear sense' (2000a:181) and that relating linguistic mental representations to things in the world is not simple and 'perhaps even a misconceived project' (1994a:159). If there is no external reality, then there is no Chomsky (and you're not reading this, either). But this sceptical conclusion, while immune to refutation, is neither fruitful nor interesting, and is clearly not what the putative Chomsky had in mind.

Rather, he is calling into question the traditional philosophical treatment of semantics in terms of a systematic word–world relation such that the word 'red' refers to red things, 'elm' refers to elm trees, 'water' refers to H_2O, and so on. Chomsky (1995a, etc.) argues at length that, although we can refer by using words, words themselves do not refer. '*People* use words to refer to things in complex ways, reflecting interests and circumstances, but the *words* do not refer' (1996:22).

The idea that words refer to things, and sentences refer to states of affairs, in the world is deeply entrenched, but misguided. The source of the misapprehension is the assumption that meaning is necessarily to be described in terms of truth, that is, the meaning of a sentence is given by its truth conditions: the set of conditions whose fulfilment would guarantee the truth of the sentence. At first blush this idea is not entirely silly: if someone asks whether the assertion that 'Scandinavians are dolichocephalic' is true, then a prerequisite to being able to answer the question is knowing what the word means ('long-headed'). That is, to say that '*Scandinavians are dolichocephalic' is true* is equivalent to saying that '*Scandinavians are long-headed' is true*, or 'Scandinavians are dolichocephalic' means that Scandinavians are long-headed. In such cases truth and meaning seem to be inter-convertible in a reasonably simple way, but there are serious problems. These problems fall into different classes and have prompted a panoply of sophisticated accretions to truth-conditional theories of meaning. Chomsky's solution is more radical: to give up on truth as relevant for I-language. Let us look first at some of the reasons for denying the word–world relation, and then at what might constitute an alternative.

One of Chomsky's favourite examples (e.g. 1993a:22, 1995a:21, 1996:22) is 'London'. It seems straightforward to say that the word 'London' refers to the city which is the capital of the UK. But Chomsky draws a distinction between our use of the word to refer to London – something which is unproblematic – and the unjustified further claim that, because we can use the word to refer, the word itself refers to some real entity in the world. London might be destroyed and rebuilt elsewhere, but it would still be London; I can refer to the same entity by using terms like 'the city where I work', 'the great wen', or indefinitely many others; or I can use the word 'London' with no referential intention at all, as when I say in exasperation 'Look, either you work in London or you don't work in London, there are no other logical possibilities.' The argument is ultimately a reflection of a disagreement about the nature of semantics. The philosophical tradition is wedded to the assumption, usually associated with the nineteenth-century philosopher Frege, that it is possible to assign truth conditions to every possible (assertoric) utterance. The alternative internalist view is that semantic relations are nothing to do with things in the world but are relations between mental representations: they are entirely inside the head. It is no more appropriate to assume that 'London' picks out a specific entity in the world than it is to postulate a real-world entity of 'nearness' which is possessed to a greater or less extent by various objects. Whether London is 'near' Birmingham is something which is determined not by facts in the real world, but by our perspective on those facts. In the context of European cartography, London and Birmingham are 'near'; in the context of the Ramblers' Association they are not. No one has suggested that 'nearness' should be assigned the status of an externally valid absolute; Chomsky's point is that standard philosophical assumptions about language and reference are equivalent to doing just that: in particular, the assumption that there are common meanings expressed in a public language (E-language) is at the root of a deep confusion.

There is an intuitive appeal to the notion that there is an external language that different people speak. Indeed, it is so self-evidently true that it would be pointless to deny it. However, when taken to its logical conclusion, the idea turns out to be problematic, as the notion of 'language' involved is different from the notion that linguists theorize about. Why? First, we all differ from each other in vocabulary: you may not have known the word 'dolichocephalic' I used earlier, and you certainly know words I don't. Within an externalist framework, this problem is not difficult to accommodate: we each know a subset of the words of the language we speak, where the totality of that vocabulary is encapsulated in major dictionaries. Matters are (supposedly) not so easy for internalists, where there is no external standard provided by a public language. Problematic examples are provided by disagreements over meaning of the kind seen in Burge's 'arthritis' (1992:217) or Putnam's twin-earth 'water'. It is supposed to be necessary to a correct understanding of 'arthritis' that there be social agreement as to what the word 'really' means; hence there has to be a public language code in which this meaning is represented. But, first, this external code doesn't obviously solve the problem of partial communication; second, there is no problem in making the simple internalist assumption that your interlocutors are like you until you get evidence that this is false, and then you modify your interpretation of their utterances accordingly. If you tell me that you have arthritis in your cheek, I shall think you ignorant of standard medical usage and interpret your hypochondria accordingly. No more needs to be said.

Similarly with twin-earth and the problems of Pierre, who is confused about whether London (which he considers ugly) is the same as Londres (which he considers beautiful). If Oscar is transported to Putnam's twin-earth and has a drink from the tap, believing it to be H_2O when in fact it is XYZ, he is mistaken, but nothing of import follows about the nature of language.

Chomsky's scepticism about 'external reality' is then best interpreted as an affirmation of the discontinuity between two perspectives on language. Specifically, his preoccupation with developing a scientific theory of the language faculty – and his ignoring for the most part of how that faculty is put to use in comprehension, and of how it is used to refer, for instance – leads him to believe that there is no role for a theory of reference *within it*: 'It is possible that natural language has only syntax and pragmatics' (1995a:26). This does not deny that humans use language to refer, but referring crucially involves going outside the language faculty. Answering the question we started with ultimately requires an understanding of Chomsky's contribution to epistemology: knowledge of language is not 'grounded' in the way conscious knowledge is traditionally supposed to be, it is there as part of our make-up as humans. Chomsky exists all right, but 'Chomsky' doesn't refer to him.

Note

This essay first appeared in 1998 in *GI* 3,1:9. I am happy to report that Chomsky still exists, and is still producing new ideas in linguistics, and renewed attacks on concentrations of power everywhere else. An overview of his ideas – linguistic, philosophical, psychological and political – can be found in Smith (1999); an excellent overview of the internalist position is provided by Segal (2000). Recent examples of Chomsky's philosophical work appear in Chomsky (2000a), of his linguistic work in Chomsky (1999a, 2000b, 2000e), and of his political work in Chomsky (1998, 1999c, 1999d, 1999e, 1999f, 1999g, 2000c, 2000d, 2000f, etc.).

All the bibliographic references in this essay are to Chomsky . . .

18

Relentless Jollity, Inexorable Logic and the Nature of Mind

Steven Pinker is a distinguished cognitive scientist who has made a major contribution to learnability theory and language acquisition. He is also a media star, whose latest book, *Words and Rules* (1999) – complete with gaudily embossed dust cover – automatically qualifies for review in both the popular and the academic press: something which makes the rest of us green with envy. He has also been known both to support and to misinterpret Chomsky on occasion (see chapter 15 above), so I had mixed feelings when I started reading. But for once, the hype is justified; this is a very good book.

Cognitive science has been preoccupied for the last fifteen years or so with a virulent dispute between those who view the mind as manipulating symbols and those who view it as (merely) a neural network of interacting connections. Classic examples of the former are provided by virtually all theories of linguistics – quintessentially by Chomsky's theory of generative grammar; examples of the latter are furnished by sundry connectionists, beginning with the pioneering contribution of Rumelhart and McClelland's (1986) theory of parallel distributed processing. For theoretical linguists, there is no hope whatsoever of capturing the infinite richness of our knowledge of language without having recourse to rules defined over symbols. For connectionists, there is no need whatsoever for either the rules or the symbols: the patterns and regularities we observe emerge automatically as a function of statistical regularities in the input to the system.

Pinker has long been associated with the symbolic camp, but in his latest book he attempts a bridge-building exercise that seeks to unite the best of both worlds. He does it with his customary flair, claiming that the issues can be illuminated, even resolved, by a sustained and detailed investigation of the properties of English regular and irregular verbs and nouns. Those who are put off by the baroque complexity of much syntactic argumentation or the perennial opacity of the mathematical underpinnings of connectionism will be surprised, and delighted, to see a conceptually complex area dissected with wit and insight on the basis of nothing more complex than the contrast between the regular *talk–talked* and the irregular *sing–sang*. Regular alternations of the first kind are produced by rules defined over symbols; irregular alternations of the second kind result from accessing words stored in an associative network in memory, with no reference to the regular rule. Both rules and association are necessary: no theory that attempts to do without rules, and no theory that attempted to rely exclusively on rules, could account for the vast array of facts that Pinker parades before us.

Evidence comes from all directions. We are regaled with a wealth of humorous and often original examples from every area you can think of: language change in history; language acquisition by little children; language breakdown in those who have suffered a stroke or other brain damage; native speaker reactions to words and sentences in a variety of experimental situations; the results of Positron Emission Tomography, functional Magnetic Resonance Imaging, Event-Related Potentials; and more. Many of his examples are familiar, but many others are new, ranging from reports on baseball games in small-town American newspapers to the novels of Jane Austen; from strip cartoons to the latest results from the professional psycholinguistic literature. And all of them are presented with a relentless jollity that is entertaining for the first few dozen examples but gradually becomes wearing. Fortunately, as he addresses deeper issues at the end of the book, the jollity rating declines accordingly.

Consider some of his examples. Neologisms like *uncheesy* and *headmistressly* could not be interpreted on the basis of information stored in memory because, in virtue of being neologisms, there can be no such stored information. So we need rules to account for them. The results of subliminal priming, where an 'invisible' stimulus like *filled* facilitates the recognition of *fill*, but a comparably invisible *rode* has no effect on the recognition of *ride*, follow from the claim that the former pair are related by rule, but the latter are stored independently in memory. The interpretation by pre-school children of *green spider eater* as ambiguous between 'a green eater of spiders' and 'an eater of green spiders', whereas *green spiders eater* is seen unambiguously as referring to 'an eater of green spiders', falls out naturally from independently motivated differences between regular and irregular forms (*green mice eater* is ambiguous – *mice* is an irregular plural, *spiders* is a regular one).

In all these cases, and hundreds of others like them, the facts can be explained on the assumption that there is a systematic distinction between regular forms produced by rule, and irregular forms retrieved ready-made from memory. More accurately, rules – for instance, that producing Pinker's favourite *moshed* from *mosh* – apply by default to any form that doesn't have an irregular congener already stored in memory; hence to all new coinages. But it is this postulation of rules, in contradistinction to the equally necessary associative network of memory, that separates theoretical linguists from their connectionist rivals. Pinker goes to great lengths to emphasize that both these elements are needed, and that the related philosophical positions of associationism and rationalism are themselves 'right about different parts of the mind'. The former allows us to account simply for the generalization of the pattern in *sing–sang–sung* to that in *bring–brang–brung*; the latter for the different generalization that turns *ploamph* into *ploamphed*.

It is not just that no connectionist network could be devised that would churn out the correct results. With suitable malice aforethought, such networks can be coerced into doing almost anything. But they are inherently unable to deal adequately with a situation where frequency does not correlate with regularity: failing to capture regularities they ought to be able to, and blithely capturing ones they should not be able to. For the former, Pinker provides the interesting example of the rare German plural in -*s*. German has eight varieties of plural formation, of which the least frequent is that seen in *Auto–Autos*. Yet this is the form that serves as the default when nothing else is to hand: for loan-words (like *Hobbys*), neologisms (like *Homepages*), members of a family (like *die Manns*), eponyms (like *Fausts*), acronyms (like *GmbHs*), and on. Connectionist networks have serious difficulty in generalizing the statistically least frequent pattern to cover new forms. Networks are explicitly devised to be sensitive to frequency and generalize the commonest patterns, not the least common.

For the latter situation, where a network sees patterns it shouldn't, I give an example from work done by Ianthi Tsimpli and me (Smith and Tsimpli 1995). We have spent some years investigating the polyglot savant Christopher, a man who is intellectually handicapped and unable to look after himself, but who can speak some twenty or so languages. To test the limits of his abilities and search for an explanation of his prodigious talent, we invented an impossible language and taught it to him and a control group of undergraduates. One 'impossible' aspect of the language involved the need to count the number of words in a sentence and then carry out some operation 'at the end of the third word'. No process in any human language is like that (it is not structure dependent), and neither the savant nor the undergraduates worked out the rule. But no connectionist network worth its salt would fail to induce such a generalization on the basis of the (plentiful) input data, and humans in puzzle-solving mode can do so as well. But in the linguistic domain we are genetically programmed not to see such regularities, because natural languages *never* exploit them. However necessary it may be in some domains, in this area, connectionism is too powerful for its own good. Not only do we need rules, but the rules we need are not even of the kind that connectionists can handle. Pinker succeeds in generating light rather than heat in a dispute that has been noted for acrimony rather than insight. This is no mean achievement but, as a bonus, he extends the argumentation to cover the nature of mind more generally, addressing the even wider debate between protagonists of prototypes and of traditional Aristotelian categories, suggesting that the human mind is a hybrid, 'learning fuzzy associations and crisp rules in different subsystems'. It seems initially implausible that meditating on the past tense of *sing* could enable one to derive generalizations about how our mental categories 'reflect the lawfulness of the world', but Pinker has done it. Hats off.

Note

This essay developed out of a review of Steven Pinker's *Words and Rules* in the *Times Literary Supplement* for 18 February 2000. The piece was entitled 'Don't only connect'. See the next chapter for a somewhat more jaundiced view of connectionism.

19

Structural Eccentricities

Is connectionism really intellectually bankrupt or does it just look like it? The question is prompted by reading *Rethinking Innateness* (Elman et al. 1996), a book I find linguistically simplistic, philosophically naïve and rhetorically dishonest. As the authors are leaders in their field and the book promises to be influential, it seems appropriate to take a hard look.

Connectionism, whether viewed as a theory of the mind (including the language faculty) or a way of implementing a Theory of the Mind, is a throwback to behaviourism of a fairly crass kind. Connectionism 'does not construe cognition as involving symbol manipulation' (Bechtel and Abrahamsen 1991:2), so there is no place for the generalizations, representations, principles or rules that are the bread and butter of linguists. Everything from the ECP to the OCP is either unnecessary or will emerge from a connectionist network without needing to be referred to.

A corollary of this view is that language is merely a skill and 'any arbitrary skill can achieve "automaticity" if it is practised often enough' (1996:386). Similarly, 'the line between learning and maturation is not obvious in any behavioral domain. Language is no exception in this regard' (1996:388). 'Grammars are complex behavioral solutions to the problem of mapping structured meanings onto a linear string of sounds' (1996:39). Linguistic universals (1996:385–6) fare little better. After discussing how a network can learn Exclusive Or and make 3-D reconstructions from 2-D representations, the authors say: 'A similar story may underlie the universals that have been reported for grammar.' *How* a similar story might work is not explained. Similarly, in earlier work cited approvingly here (1996:343ff), Elman (1993) trained a network on increasingly complex sentences of the form exemplified in (1):

1. Boy chases dog
    Boys chase dog
    Mary walks
    Boy who dogs chase feeds cat
    Girls who chases dogs hits cats [*sic*]

Elman wanted to demonstrate that a network would learn better if the data it was taught on increased gradually in complexity, replicating the kind of maturational change characteristic of children. Unfortunately, the network needed training on half a million sentences in order to learn the relevant patterns; complexity was modulated by decreasing the short-term memory of the system – that is, not a linguistic variable – and 'the fully complex data set' exemplified in (1) lacks precisely those linguistic properties which are of greatest interest – functional categories, like *the* and *a*.

Philosophically the situation is even worse. 'We define knowledge in terms of fine-grained connectivity at the cortical level' (1996:314), and 'knowledge ultimately refers to a specific pattern of synaptic connections in the brain' (1996:359). This is reductionist twaddle. Knowledge may be ultimately *realized* by such a pattern, but it is 'ultimately' a specific pattern of elementary particles interacting in eleven dimensions. The level of discussion is as misconceived in one case as it would be in the other.

Discussion of poverty-of-the-stimulus arguments is comparable, and in Bates and Elman (1996:1849) even more blatant: 'There are, in fact, a number of ways to get round [*sic*] the poverty-of-the-stimulus argument. First, we could relax our definition of knowledge, defining successful learning to include behavior that is asymptotically correct but somewhere short of perfect . . . Second, we could base our estimates of learnability on a more robust learning device than the one assumed by Chomsky . . . Third, . . .'. But it's not worth continuing, so let me quote their account of modularity, specifically whether there is evidence for the domain-specificity characteristic of modules. Looking at the rather special properties of the language faculty they comment that 'the mere existence of structural eccentricities tells us little about . . . their domain-specific or domain-general character' (1996:384). 'Structural eccentricities' turn out to be syntax.

Despite this apparent jettisoning of a rather healthy baby with some murky bath-water, perhaps connectionism has some properties which it would be desirable to preserve. It has at least eight characteristics that its protagonists take to indicate its superiority to other approaches: it is explicit, interactive, statistically based, 'plastic', self-organizing, it manifests graceful degradation, it has neural correlates, and it lays emphasis on timing (that is, the epigenetic unfolding of species characteristics rather than their simple genetic determination).

Some of these properties are more desirable than others: having neural correlates is as empty as having superstring correlates. One can have no objection to explicitness, but there is no difference here between connectionism and formal grammar or any symbol-based implementation of such a grammar. How far a theory of language should be 'interactive' is an empirical question. There are interesting issues on the relation between input systems, modules, quasi-modules and so on, but this literature is not discussed. The claim that networks are self-organizing is probably false: given a massive input, particular patterns reminiscent of natural-language categories emerge, but to reproduce human judgements with any degree of sophistication requires building in particular weightings on the connections: that is, providing 'innate' structure. The putative advantage of emphasizing the importance of timing is unclear, as it is never explained why unique timing developments should be any the less under genetic control than location or cell type.

Connectionism prides itself on being statistically based. This is not an unmixed blessing. Frequency does have a measurable effect on response latencies to lexical items, judgements of prototypicality, and so on, but such performance regularities can be captured statistically by many systems. Humans are good at one-off learning and do not need the massive exposure to patterns that is characteristic of connectionist networks. Moreover, and more importantly, as we saw in the previous chapter, there are statistical regularities that humans are *in*sensitive to.

The Principle of Structure Dependence applies universally to natural languages, but not to connectionist networks. In Smith and Tsimpli (1995; see also Smith et al. 1993) we demonstrated that subjects were unable to learn a structure-independent rule of emphasis formation: something a network could do with ease. Elman (1993:87) gives the example of the array in (2), where the 0 or 1 in the right-hand column is a function of the properties of the sequence in the left-hand column:

2. 1 0 1 1 0 1   1
    0 0 0 0 0 0   1
    0 0 1 1 0 0   1
    0 1 0 1 1 0   0
    1 1 1 0 1 1   0
    0 0 0 1 1 1   0

and asks what the network would do with the sequence in (3):

3. 0 1 1 1 0 1   ?

He suggests various possible hypotheses that might be tested to determine whether you complete (3) with a 0 or a 1: whether the display is symmetrical about the centre, whether it manifests even parity, whether 1 occurs in fifth position. All of these are counting algorithms rather than structure dependent ones, and grammars can't count. *Structure depend-ence is the prerequisite to, not the outcome of, language acquisition.* It is possible to tweak a network so that it could not learn structure-independent operations, correctly replicating the behaviour of human subjects. But such manipulation requires building in the 'innate' structure that is anathema to con-nectionists. The problem is acute because humans *are* capable of identifying such patterns in the context of a puzzle, but not apparently in the context of language learning. Demarc-ating such different domains is precisely what any version of the modularity hypothesis is designed to do.

The property of 'graceful degradation' is interesting, but still represents a dubious advantage. Consider the phenom-enon of 'retreat', where a child who has internalized a gram-mar which over-generates, giving examples like Bowerman's (1987) 'don't giggle me', retreats to a grammar in which this is, correctly, ungrammatical. According to Elman, gradient descent 'makes it difficult for a network to make dramatic changes in its hypotheses. Once a network is committed to an erroneous generalisation it may be unable to escape' (Elman 1993:94). This makes the problem of retreat insoluble.

Plasticity, the fact that 'region x can be co-opted to carry out the function usually effected by region y', is used as an argument against modular systems. The idea is that the claimed innateness of modularity is undermined by the brain's ability to compensate for injury in one area by 'redeploying' its forces. If a child suffers damage to the language area (for example, in the form of a left hemispherectomy) the lan-guage function may be taken over by the right hemisphere. It is supposed to follow that modularity cannot be prespecified. But it is not clear why there is even a problem: the very notion of plasticity presupposes that regions x and y are, in the absence of pathological conditions, pre-specified for par-ticular (modular) functions.

Does connectionism have anything to offer the linguist? It has one useful role to play: spelling out precisely what consti-tutes a good poverty-of-the-stimulus argument. Linguists tend to adduce such arguments blithely, even irresponsibly, in defence of innateness claims. What connectionist networks can do is show the extent to which such claims are really justified. But otherwise? The answer is not much. Linguists are not likely to derive much benefit from a model that relegates syntax to the status of 'structural eccentricities'.

Note

This essay first appeared in 1997 in *GI* 2,8:7. The debate – or battle – between symbolists and connectionists continues to rage. See chapter 18 above for a review of Pinker's recent book trying to reconcile the two positions, with a much more positive evaluation of connectionist theories. Representative examples of the debate include: Fodor (2000); Grossberg (2000); and Schlottmann (2000). A recent book by Peter Culicover (1999) attempts *inter alia* to show that even e.g. parasitic gaps do not constitute a good poverty-of-the-stimulus argument.

20

The Velarity of Linguists

Linguists begin with velars. Consider Kager, Katz, Kaye, Kayne, Keenan, Kempson, Kenstowicz, Kim, Kiparsky, Kisseberth, Klima, (van de) Koot, Koster and Kuno (not to mention Carnie, Carston, Clark, Clements, Comrie and Cormack). Some are voiced: Gazdar, Givón, Gleitman, Goldsmith, Gopnik, Gorrell and Greenberg; and as a brief glance at the LSA *Bulletin* confirms, one or two are even nasal: Ng and Nguyen for instance. I assume that this is not too controversial, but I intended my opening sentence to have universal force. *All* linguists begin with velars. So either you begin with a velar or you're not a linguist.

I suspect that by now you are slightly sceptical. What about Chomsky and Halle? Most people take them to be linguists. But of course, their names do begin with velars. If you refer to the Russian literature you will find that Chomsky always appears as Xomsky – a perfect initial velar fricative – and given that *Hamlet* turns up in Russian as *Gamlet*, we shouldn't have much trouble with Morris either. Anyway, every Greek pronounces Halle with an initial velar scrape, so the authors of *The Sound Pattern of English* (1968) aren't counter-examples to my claim. And parity of argument suggests that we can now accommodate Cheng, Cinque and Chao; Hale, Haegeman, Harris and Hudson; in the same way.

There is in fact a long tradition which recognizes the systematic relation between velars and each of palato-alveolars and glottals by deriving the latter from the former: Italian *amico* and *amici*, or the etymologically related pairs *canine* and *hound* or *guest* and *host*, are cases in point. Germanic [h] generally corresponds to Indo-European – for instance, Sanskrit – [k], so these are not isolated examples. On the further assumption that voicing is generally irrelevant to point of articulation, we can probably sneak in Giorgi, Jackendoff and Joos; Johnson, Jones and Jusczyk; as well.

As my appeal to etymology suggests, this pervasive velarity is best revealed in diachronic developments: everyone recognizes the relationship between Latin *centum* and Italian *cento*, so deriving one from the other synchronically is not a problem. But this step suggests that we can now extend the opening claim to some more linguisticky people. While Latin has [k] in *caput* or *caballus*, French has [ʃ] in *chef* and *cheval*, so this potentially brings Schachter, Schane, Schwartz and Shieber into the fold. The hypothesis is looking good.

I must admit that my own name might be viewed as slightly problematic. The first part is easy: 'Neil' obviously derives from the homophonous form 'kneel', where the velar onset is overt, albeit silent. Suitably reconstructed then I can lay claim to being partially a linguist. But 'Smith'? Well, we could simply use as a tool the etymological relatedness of Latin [k] to modern [s] – as in the French (and English) *cent*; or we could invoke the pervasive effects of velar softening as seen in the alternation between *electric* and *electricity*; but it's probably helpful to use an alternative, slightly longer, derivation in corroboration. Consider Andalucian Spanish, where preconsonantal [s] typically becomes [h], so that Castilian 'las moscas' is pronounced [lah mohkah]. As we have already established the relationship between [h] and [k], the extra step is immediately plausible: *Smith* comes from 'Kmith' via 'Hmith'. In fact my son provided evidence of this intervening stage at the age of 2 when he systematically pronounced words like *smoke* and *Smith* as 'hmok' and 'hmith' (actually [m̥ok] and [m̥it]), so it may well be that the velarity of linguists is innate. At any rate, we can now account for a wealth of professional sibilant talent from Sag to Sybesma, with Sapir, Siegel, Slobin, Speas and Strozer picked up en route.

What about the labials, which might appear superficially difficult for the hypothesis? Here there is good evidence from the languages of West Africa that their non-coronality is really velarity in disguise. Yoruba orthographic 'p' is pronounced [kp] (and anyway [p] alternates with [k] in a number of Amerindian languages), so we can rescue the benighted labials from the danger of linguistic exclusion, bringing in Pinker, Plank and Postal, even Prince, Partee, Perlmutter and Pullum. But on this argument extending the analysis to the voiced labials is a little vexed. As the name of the Yoruba linguist Bamgbose indicates, his language does have a contrast between [b] and [gb]. In his particular case, there is no problem – his name clearly involves metathesis: *Bamgbose* is underlyingly *Gbambose*; but we need a better solution for the others. Another West African language provides relevant evidence. In Fula there is a complex system of consonant mutation, reminiscent of that in the Celtic languages, whereby [g] alternates with [w] for one class of verbs, and [w] alternates with [b] for another class. The moral should be obvious: 'b' and 'm' are cryptic encodings of velarity, so we can now include Bach, Basbøll, Bresnan, Brody and Bolinger, as well as Macken, Manzini, May, Moravcsik and Morgan, in our pantheon. Indeed the bi-directional alternation seen in Fula allows us to extend the title of linguist to our labio-velar colleagues Wang, Wilson and Whorf; Weinberg, Wells and Winograd; as well. Success is at hand.

However, I have so far managed to encompass only a small subset of the coronal linguists, traditionally the richest tribe. Some of the remainder succumb easily to the same kind of treatment as given above. The alternation in Spanish between [k] and [θ], as in *dico* and *dice*, makes the inclusion of Thornton, Thurgood and Thrainsson possible in a single simple step. Other alveolars are less obvious, but it is surely not accidental that in Slavic [ts] and [dz] derive from velar stops, nor that in Fox [t] alternates with [tʃ]. If [tʃ] derives from [k] as we have seen above, and if [t] alternates with [tʃ], we are home and dry with Talmy, Teeter and Terzi, not to mention Toribio, Tenny and Tranel. On the usual assumptions about voicing, that also licenses Dell, Derwing and Dinnsen, as well as Dresher, Dressler and half the French aristocracy; though whether it really justifies us in including Neidle, Nespor and Neeleman, or Newmark and Newmeyer, is moot. Maybe we can treat them as we did 'Neil' a little while ago, or we could invoke the phenomenon of consonant harmony. Children, with their usual preternatural ability, often pronounce words better than their misguided elders: [gakman] rather than *Drachman*, [ŋagase] for *Nagase*. We still have a little way to go, but the end is in sight. Labio-dentals might be considered a problem, and we obviously don't want to exclude Fabb, Flickinger or Fromkin, and it is *essential* to include sundry Fodors and Fowlers. Relax, alternation will come to our rescue again. Consider the systematic relation between 'f' and 'p' in English: we have *foot* and *pedestrian, father* and *paternal, full* and *plenary.* It is evident that [f] derives from [p], and as [p] in turn derives from [k] through the intermediate stage of [kp], our colleagues are not lost, and even Vergnaud and Verkuyl, Varlokosta and Vincent, can be invited to the velar party.

There are two remaining problems: (putative) linguists who begin with vowels, and those who begin with liquids. The latter are easy: alternations between [l] and [ɫ] (the 'dark' velarized allophone) are familiar to everyone, so the choice of an anomalous pronunciation for their names by some people – *Ladd* and *Levin* pronounced as [lad] and [levin] rather than [ɫad] or [ɫevin] – is just due to obstinacy, or a failure to realize the implications of their choice. 'R' too is subject to a range of alternative quasi-velar realizations, as in the Northumberland 'burr', and if this is not convincing evidence of their inherent velarity (or uvularity), there is always the possibility of an alternative appeal to rhotacism: the alternation of [r] with [s] (as in Latin *flos/floris*). We've already seen that [s] can be derived from a velar, and now we see that [r] can be derived from [s]. So welcome Rauch, Roberts and Roussou, Rivero, Rosen and Ross.

The metonymic vowels, from Aarts to Unger, Epstein to Ojeda, Ito to Yngve, can be similarly accommodated once you remember the conventions for alliteration in earlier Germanic verse. It used to be a puzzle that words beginning with one vowel could alliterate with words beginning with any other vowel, until it was realized that all such words really began with a glottal stop, and that alliteration was defined in terms of this consonantal onset. But now it is simple: we have already seen that glottals are related to velars, so all these vocalic people are safe, and Adger and Ash are underlyingly really 'Cadger' and 'Cash'.

So there we are – velar. All of us. Just a few observations to round things off. First, it might be thought that there was a moral about the evil of abstractness, or the dangers of derivational complexity, or the horror of massive under-specification to be drawn from this scholarly discussion of onomasiology. Perish the thought. We need constraints, but I have rarely felt less moralistic, and all Voltairean conclusions are drawn at your own risk. Second, this is the first (and last) article in which I have managed to mention *all* my colleagues: that should help in the next research assessment exercise. Finally, it might be objected that my claim of velarity is unscientific because it is unfalsifiable. This is not true. Note that implicit in the foregoing are two empirical hypotheses: first, no linguist begins with [ð] (Spanish has no alternation between [g] and [ð], for instance, parallel to that between [k] and [θ]). Given the current upsurge in Icelandic linguistics this is clearly a testable and provocative claim. Second, it assimilates almost everyone in the world, maybe even connectionists, into the class of linguists. But this is surprisingly a desirable outcome: language is after all a property of the species, so up to (connectionist) pathology we should expect universal membership in the category. Linguists *are* velar.

Note

This essay first appeared in 1999 in *GI* 4,1:10. Various linguists have tried to assure me that their names do not begin with a velar – Moira Yip, for instance. They are, of course, deluded.

Glossary

Words in **bold** within entries refer you to other entries.

adjunction A syntactic process which creates a new node in a tree, such that this new node is identical to the one it is attached to.

agnosia The loss, usually as the result of brain damage, of the ability to recognize or perceive familiar stimuli.

algorithm A computational procedure which is guaranteed to solve a particular problem.

amusia The loss, usually as the result of brain damage, of the ability to recognize or perceive musical stimuli.

anencephalic Born without (part of) the brain.

aphasia Loss of language as a result of brain damage.

apraxia Impaired ability to carry out deliberate physical movements.

ASL American Sign Language. The language of the American deaf community.

binding That part of linguistic theory that deals with relations between noun phrases and their linguistic antecedents. In *Fred admires himself,* the word *himself* is bound by the noun phrase *Fred. See also* **NP**.

BSL British Sign Language. The language of the British deaf community.

calendrical calculator A savant whose talent resides in the ability to tell immediately on which day of the year any date, past or future, falls.

categorial perception   The perception of physically different stimuli, such as 'p' and 'b', as belonging to different categories. New-born infants are able to make many such discriminations.

central system   That part of the mind devoted to problem solving and the fixation of belief.

code   A systematic relation between form and meaning, such as the 's' in *cats* encoding plurality. *See also* **inference**.

comparative   A linguistic form used to represent comparison: e.g. *bigger than*.

competence   Knowledge of language.

conjunction   Grammatical linking of words or phrases by means of items such as *and* or *while*.

connectionism   A psychological theory that attempts to reduce thought and other cognitive processes to connections between (models of) brain cells.

conservation   In Piagetian psychology, the ability to recognize, for instance, that an amount of liquid poured from a short fat container into a tall thin container remains the same.

constituent   In **syntax**, a group of words that form a structural unit. Technically, a sequence of items that can be traced exhaustively to a single **node** in a **tree**.

constructivism   The psychological position that cognition is constructed from an undifferentiated mind. *Contrast* **modularity**.

contextual effect   In Relevance Theory, when an utterance is interpreted in some context, it may have any of a variety of effects: for instance, it may strengthen some of your assumptions, or it may contradict them, leading you to revise your view.

control   That part of linguistic theory that deals with relations between noun phrases and an understood (**empty**) **category**. For example, in *John promised Mary to behave himself*, the empty subject of 'to behave', called 'PRO', is (i.e. is controlled by) *John*; in *John told Mary to behave herself*, the empty subject of 'to behave' is (i.e. is controlled by) *Mary*. *See also* **NP**.

coordination A kind of **conjunction** in which two or more items linked by an element such as *and* have the same syntactic status.

coronal A consonant articulated with the tip or front of the tongue: e.g. 't', 'd', 's', 'l' in English.

cortex The outer layer of the brain; responsible for most higher functions, such as thought, vision and language.

decode To work out the linguistic meaning of an utterance. For example, hearing *He left early*, you can decode the message that some male left at some time. You then use your pragmatic (inferential) ability to work out which male left, and when precisely he did so.

deep structure In early (transformational) **generative** grammar, a level of syntactic representation which was the output of the Phrase Structure rules and the input to **transformations**. It was designed to capture regularities, such as that *John* has the same interpretation in both *John was tricked* and *Someone tricked John*, despite the different positions in which it occurs. *See also* **syntax, surface structure**.

dependency A relation in which a grammatical element is governed by another. For example, in the sentence *John thinks that he is a werewolf*, the clause *that he is a werewolf* depends on (is a dependent of) the verb *thinks*.

diachronic Pertaining to development through time, as in historical (or 'diachronic') linguistics. *See also* **synchronic**.

discrete infinity The property of human language of having an infinity of sentences, each of which is constructed out of discrete individual parts (e.g. words and phrases). This property is shared with the number system.

dissociation 1 The independence of two functions, such as sight and hearing, and hence their separate susceptibility to pathological breakdown in blindness and deafness.

dissociation 2 In **pragmatics**, the distancing or separation of one's own view from that which is being entertained. For instance, in irony, one typically dissociates oneself from what is being said.

Down syndrome   A chromosomal abnormality (typically Trisomy 21) leading to physical and mental disability.

E-language   Human language viewed not as a psychological construct, but as a set of sentences existing in the public domain, independently of particular individuals. *See also* **I-language**.

ECP   The **Empty Category** Principle: a grammatical principle (empty categories must be properly governed) designed to constrain the proliferation of empty categories.

empty category   A grammatical category which has syntactic and semantic properties but is not pronounced; as the understood subject 'you' in *Leave me alone*; or the PRO subject of *elope* in *John wants to elope. See also* **control**.

ERP   Event-Related Potential: components of the brain's electrical activity. Particular wave-forms are characteristic of specific linguistic stimuli; e.g. the difference between syntactic deviance, as in *the children fries an egg*, and semantic anomaly, as in *the children fried a carpet*.

externalism   The view that language exists external to the individuals who speak it. *Contrast* **internalism**.

false belief   The ability, which develops at about 4 years of age, to understand that other people can have views which differ from your own (and from reality). The ability is central to the **Theory of Mind**, and is characteristically lacking in autistic subjects.

fMRI   Functional Magnetic Resonance Imaging. A technique for monitoring brain activity by measuring the oxygenation of blood in a magnetic field, while the subject carries out particular tasks.

focusing   A grammatical process, either syntactic or phonological, which highlights a particular constituent, typically in answer to a question. The item *bats* is focused in each of the answers to the question 'What did Mary write a book about?' Answer 1: 'She wrote a book about *bats*'; Answer 2: '*Bats*, Mary wrote a book about'.

functional category   A category which includes articles, tense, complementizers and prepositions, and excludes Nouns,

Verbs and Adjectives. Functional categories and their properties are the major source of differences among the languages of the world.

generative A grammar is generative if it uses an explicit set of formal rules and principles to characterize ('generate') the sentences or other constituents of a language.

glottal A sound like 'h' in English, or the Cockney replacement for 't' in *wa'er*, where the main articulation is at the glottis (Adam's apple).

head In **syntax**, the main constituent of a phrase on which others are dependent: for example, the verb *admire* is the head of the **verb phrase** *admire penguins*.

I-language Knowledge of language. Language viewed as a construct *internal* to the mind of the *individual*. The technical term for **competence**. *See also* **E-language**.

imaging Any of a variety of techniques for monitoring the activity of the brain. *See also* **ERP, fMRI, PET scan**.

implicature In **pragmatics**, an assumption which is communicated, but not explicitly communicated. The utterance *You've already eaten three cakes* has as one possible implicature that the addressee should not eat a fourth cake.

inference That stage in the interpretation of utterances which relies on logical processes outside the grammar (i.e. in the **central system**). Given an utterance such as *It's nearly dead*, you **decode** the message that some entity is close to death, and then infer that the 'it' refers to the family pet, you should call the vet, or tell your spouse not to exaggerate, etc.

informational encapsulation The claim, made famous by Jerry Fodor (1983), that the internal workings of **modules** (such as vision, hearing and language) are not sensitive to knowledge from the **central system**. So knowing that a visual illusion *is* an illusion doesn't stop your (encapsulated) visual system from seeing it *as* an illusion. *Contrast* **quasi-module**; *see also* **modularity**.

input system Those components of the mind/brain which feed the **central system** with information. They correspond to the senses (sight, hearing, touch, etc.) and, for some, language.

internalism   The view that languages, and in particular the meanings of words, are internal to the minds of individuals. A corollary of the position is that words as such do not refer to entities in the external world, even though humans may *use* words to refer to such entities. *Contrast* **externalism**.

interpretive use   The use of an utterance to represent some state of affairs indirectly as an 'interpration' of a thought of someone other than the speaker. The ironical use of *He's a genius* is interpretive in this sense.

intersective   An intersective adjective is one whose meaning combines simply with the meaning of the noun it modifies: *a sparkling diamond* (where *sparkling* is intersective) is both sparkling and a diamond, whereas *a fake diamond* (where *fake* is non-intersective) is fake but not a diamond.

labial   A speech sound, such as 'p' or 'b', whose major point of articulation is the lips.

labio-dental   A speech sound, such as 'f' or 'v', whose major point of articulation involves contact between the lips and the teeth.

landing-site   A position to which some **constituent** can be moved by a grammatical rule.

language of thought   The representational system used by the mind in thinking. It is similar, but not identical, to natural human languages, whether signed or spoken. Also called 'mentalese'.

laryngeal   Pertaining to the larynx (glottis), and sounds articulated there. The difference between voiced and unvoiced sounds, such as 'b' and 'p', depends on the vibration of the vocal cords in the larynx. *See also* **voicing**.

lexical   To do with the lexicon, the (mentally represented and stored) vocabulary of one's language.

manifest (mutually)   In **pragmatics**, a fact is manifest if it is capable of being mentally represented at the time concerned; it is mutually manifest if both speaker and hearer are able to represent it. For instance, if you are with a friend and the phone rings, it is normally mutually manifest that this is the case.

metalinguistic negation The use of negation to deny not the truth of a proposition but the form in which it has been encoded. The utterance *He's not tall, he's a giant* does not deny that he is tall, but objects to the mildness of the characterization.

metarepresentation The representation of a representation, as in the use of irony.

modularity The claim that cognition is compartmentalized such that the mind consists of a set of modules (such as vision, language, number, music, moral judgement), each of which is in part independent of the others, can operate autonomously, and can break down idiosyncratically. Views on modularity are extremely diverse and all of them are controversial. *Contrast* **constructivism**.

morpho-lexical To do with the morphology and lexicon of the language. *See* **morphological, lexical**.

morphological To do with the internal structure of words; for instance, the word 'transformations' is composed of the elements 'transform', '-ation' and '-s', and even 'transform' can be broken down into 'trans' and 'form'.

movement The displacement of some item from the position where it is understood. In *John was kissed by a mermaid* and *She kissed John passionately*, the item *John* is interpreted in much the same way in both sentences: i.e. as undergoing an act of kissing. It is said to have moved to the front of the sentence in the first of the examples.

MRI *See* fMRI.

mutation A process whereby the initial consonant of a word changes under particular phonological or grammatical conditions. In Welsh, the word for 'father' is <u>t</u>ad, but 'your father' is dy <u>d</u>ad, 'her father' is ei <u>th</u>ad, and 'my father' is fy <u>nh</u>ad. *See also* **phonology**.

nasal A speech sound, such as 'm' or 'n' in English, which is pronounced with passage of air through the nose.

neologism A newly coined word or phrase, such as (*previously*) *unencounterable*.

node Any point in a **tree** from which a branch (i.e. a line) emanates.

NP   Noun phrase, exemplified by such constituents as *John, the penguin, all my friends*, etc.

OCP   The Obligatory Contour Principle. A principle of **phonology** which prohibits adjacent occurrences of the same element.

onomasiology   The study of proper names.

over-generalization   The extension of a linguistic pattern to inappropriate items: for instance, the replacement – typical of little children – of *ran* by 'runned'.

palato-alveolar   A consonant, such as 'ch' in English 'church', articulated with the front of the tongue raised towards the hard palate, and the tip or blade of the tongue in contact with the alveolar ridge.

paradigm   The set of all the inflected forms of a word. An English example is provided by the verb *kiss*, with its forms *kisses, kissed* and *kissing*. In many languages, paradigms can have hundreds or even thousands of different forms.

parameter   *See* **principles and parameters**.

parasitic gap   A construction, exemplified by *This is the book that I reviewed * without reading *,* which contains two empty categories (indicated by the asterisks), one of which is said to be parasitic on the other.

passive   A construction, exemplified by *the hedgehog was squashed by the tractor*, in which the object (*the hedgehog*) of the verb (*squash*) is put in subject position.

PET scan   Positron Emission Tomography. A technique for investigating brain function, in which the subject is injected with radioactive liquid and the emission of positrons in the brain is monitored to see where activity is greatest.

phonology   That part of linguistic theory that deals with the sound systems and sound structures of language.

polarity items   Words such as *ever* and *any* that need to be licensed by a preceding negative (or question, etc.). Thus, it is possible to say *Has he ever been there?* and *He hasn't ever been there*; but it is ungrammatical to say *He has ever been there*.

pragmatics   The study of the interpretation of utterances. It presupposes a linguistic analysis of the sentences to which those utterances correspond.

pre-functional A stage in first-language acquisition before the child has developed any **functional categories**.

priming A psychological technique in which the speed of response to a particular stimulus is increased by 'priming' the subject with a related word. For instance, if you are asked to press a key on the computer as soon as you see the word *queen*, you will react faster if you have just seen *king* than if you have just seen *ink*, or had no previous input. *King* is then said to 'prime' *queen*.

primordia Biological organs in their earliest stage of development.

principles and parameters A major theory in current **generative** linguistics. Linguistic theory is said to consist of a set of universal *principles*, such as the principle of '**structure dependence**', and a number of *parameters*: choice points which characterize the differences among languages, such as whether they are **pro-drop** or not. In recent versions of the theory, parameters are restricted to properties of **functional categories**. First-language acquisition consists in large part of the child 'setting the parameters' of the language or languages to which he or she is exposed.

pro-drop The property, characteristic of Spanish, Greek and many other languages, of allowing subject pronouns to be omitted. In Spanish, one can say either *ella baila bien* ('she dances well') or *baila bien* ('dances well'), whereas in English only the former is possible as a complete sentence.

pronominalization The process whereby a full noun phrase, such as *the penguin*, is replaced by the equivalent pronoun, in this case *it*. For example: *I saw the penguin and bought it*.

prototype The best or most typical example of a category. A prototypical bird is a robin or a thrush, rather than an ostrich or a kiwi. Prototypes, rather than a set of necessary and sufficient conditions, are sometimes used as the basis for the meaning of words.

quasi-module A component of the mind that has some of the properties of **input systems**, but which operates on a conceptual rather than a perceptual vocabulary and is not informationally encapsulated. *Contrast* **informational encapsulation**; *see also* **modularity**.

reference   The relation, if any, between words (and other linguistic expressions) and things (and states of affairs) in the world.

reflexives   Items such as *myself, himself, themselves* which are dependent for their interpretation on a preceding linguistic item, the antecedent. *The girl hurt herself* is well formed, as *the girl* acts as the antecedent of *herself*, but *You hurt herself* is ungrammatical, as *you* is not an appropriate antecedent for *herself*.

relative clause   A clause which is part of a noun phrase and of which it modifies the **head**: e.g. *which laid an egg* in *The penguin which laid an egg is moulting*.

relevance   An utterance is relevant if it has contextual effects in some context. Other things being equal, the greater the contextual effects and the smaller the processing effort involved, the greater the relevance.

scan   One of a number of techniques for monitoring brain activity. *See* **PET scan, fMRI, ERP**.

select   To require the presence of a particular syntactic or semantic category: an auxiliary verb, such as *might*, selects, i.e. must be followed by, a main verb, such as *elope* (rather than a noun, such as *elopement*). Hence: *the lovers might elope* is grammatical, but *the lovers might elopement* is ungrammatical. *See also* **syntax, semantics**.

semantics   The study of meaning.

seriation   In Piagetian psychology, the ability to put a set of lines of different length into correct ascending or descending order.

sibilant   Any speech sound, such as 's', 'z' or 'sh', pronounced with a hissing sound.

slash category   A category with an element missing. In 'this is the book we believe *John read*', the sequence 'John read' is a sentence with a missing noun phrase (actually 'the book', which shows up earlier). Such categories are standardly written with a slash preceding the missing element; in this case: 'S/NP'.

structure dependence   All syntactic rules in all languages operate on structures rather than on unstructured strings of words. For example, to form a question in English one moves the auxiliary to the left of the subject noun phrase, deriving e.g. *Has the postman been?* from *The postman has been.* It is not possible for any human language to have a rule that moves 'the third word from the left', or that exchanges the second and fifth words. In brief, rules of grammar cannot count.

subordination   A clause which is dependent on another **constituent**, as in the bracketed parts of: *I want [John to go]* or *I love her [because she breeds alligators]* is subordinate. *See also* **dependency**.

surface structure   In early (transformational) **generative** grammar, that level of syntactic representation which was the output of the transformations. See also **deep structure**.

synaesthesia   The experiencing of one sense in terms of another, as when one hears colours or tastes sounds.

synchronic   Pertaining to the study (of language) at a single point in time, as opposed to historically. *See also* **diachronic**.

syntax   The branch of linguistics that deals with the arrangement of words in a sentence.

tag question   A clause, added to the end of a statement or order, to solicit the hearer's compliance or agreement. For example, in *It's snowing again, isn't it?*, the tag *isn't it?* turns the statement into a question.

TEFL   Teaching of English as a Foreign Language: one of the main concerns of applied linguistics.

TESL   Teaching of English as a Second Language: one of the main concerns of applied linguistics.

that-**trace**   A syntactic constraint which prohibits the occurrence of *that* next to a trace (an **empty category**). It accounts for the contrasting acceptability in English of such examples as *Who do you think came?* and the ungrammatical *Who do you think that came?*

Theory of Mind   A module of the mind that allows us to entertain the possibility that other people have minds just as we do. It enables us to infer what others are thinking in order to explain and predict their behaviour. It might more accurately be called a Theory of Other Minds. *See also* **modularity**.

theta-role   The semantic role associated with the arguments of a verb. For example, *walk* requires a noun phrase with the role of 'agent', *kiss* requires noun phrases with the roles of 'agent' and 'patient'. *See also* **NP**.

topicalization   A syntactic process which highlights the entity that the sentence is about, typically by moving it to the front of the sentence. In *Linguistics, this book is about,* the word *Linguistics* has been topicalized. *See also* **syntax**.

TP   Tense phrase. A functional category which, in recent versions of **generative** grammar, has largely taken over the role of 'Sentence'.

trace   An **empty category** marking the place from which a **constituent** has been moved.

transformation   A grammatical rule which converts one structure into another by moving some **constituent**. In earlier versions of **generative** grammar, transformations converted **deep structures** into **surface structures**.

tree   A diagrammatic representation of the **constituent** structure of a sentence.

truth conditions   Those conditions which must obtain in the real world for a sentence to report a true state of affairs. Widely used by philosophers as the basis for a theory of meaning.

UG   Universal Grammar. The innate endowment that the new-born child brings to the task of acquiring its first language. It consists of a set of principles and a number of parameters that the child fixes on the basis of exposure to incoming linguistic stimuli. *See also* **principles and parameters**.

ultimate attainment   A semi-technical term used to refer to the knowledge of a second language attained by adult learners. With a few rare exceptions, it is never quite as good as the knowledge of those who have acquired the same language as a first language.

uvular Any speech sound articulated with contact between the uvula and the back of the tongue: e.g. the '*r*' in Parisian French.

velar Any speech sound articulated with contact between the velum and the back of the tongue: e.g. '*k*', '*g*' and '*ng*' in English.

voicing The property of speech sounds articulated with vibration of the vocal cords.

VOT Voice Onset Time. The moment at which **voicing** begins in the articulation of a syllable whose initial element may be 'voiced' or 'voiceless'. That is, 'pat' and 'bat' are distinguished not only by the presence or absence of voicing in the first element, but also by the time that voicing commences.

VP Verb phrase, exemplified by such constituents as *eat a haddock, play with the children,* etc.

wh-island Clauses introduced by a wh-word, such as *whether, who, what, which,* are 'islands' in that they do not allow **constituents** to be moved from them. Thus it is possible to say either *I know the children are coming* or *I know whether the children are coming;* but while it is grammatical to say *Which children do you know are coming?,* it is ungrammatical to say: *Which children do you know whether are coming?*

Williams syndrome A condition (infantile hypercalcaemia) in which children have a variety of genetically conditioned physical characteristics and severely impoverished intellectual capacity, but extremely fluent language.

References

Adger, D., S. Pintzuk, B. Plunkett and G. Tsoulas (eds) (1999) *Specifiers: Minimalist Approaches*. Oxford, Oxford University Press.

Aitchison, J. (1998) *The Articulate Mammal*. 4th edn. London, Routledge.

Allen, W. (1975) *Without Feathers*. New York, Random House.

Asher, R. (ed.) (1994) *The Encyclopaedia of Language and Linguistics*. Oxford, Pergamon Press.

Baldwin, J. and P. French (1990) *Forensic Phonetics*. London, Pinter.

Baron-Cohen, S. (1995) *Mindblindness*. Cambridge, MA, MIT Press.

Baron-Cohen, S. and J. Harrison (eds) (1997) *Synaesthesia*. Oxford, Blackwell.

Bates, E. and J. Elman (1996) 'Learning rediscovered'. *Science* 274:1849–50.

Bechtel, W. and A. Abrahamsen (1991) *Connectionism and the Mind: An Introduction to Parallel Processing in Networks*. Oxford, Blackwell.

Bellugi, U., S. Marks, A. Bihrle and H. Sabo (1993) 'Dissociation between language and cognitive functions in Williams Syndrome'. In D. Bishop and K. Mogford (eds) *Language Development in Exceptional Circumstances*. Hillsdale, NJ, Lawrence Erlbaum. Pp. 177–89.

Berlin, B. and P. Kay (1969) *Basic Color Terms: Their Universality and Evolution*. Berkeley, CA, University of California Press.

Bernières, Louis de (1990) *The War of Don Emmanuel's Nether Parts*. London, Minerva.

Blanken, G., J. Dittmann, H. Grimm, J. Marshall and C.-W. Wallesch (eds) (1993) *Linguistic Disorders and Pathologies: An International Handbook*. Berlin, Walter de Gruyter.

Bloom, P. and L. Markson (1998) 'Capacities underlying word learning'. *Trends in Cognitive Sciences* 2,2:67–73.

Borsley, R. and R. Ingham (in press) 'Grow your own linguistics'. *Lingua.*

Bowerman, M. (1987) 'The "no negative evidence" problem: How do children avoid constructing an overly general grammar?'. In J. Hawkins (ed.) *Explaining Language Universals.* Oxford, Blackwell. Pp. 73–101.

Bregman, A. (1990) *Auditory Scene Analysis: The Perceptual Organization of Sound.* Cambridge, MA, MIT Press.

Brody, M. (1997) 'Mirror theory'. *University College London Working Papers in Linguistics* 9:179–222.

Brody, M. (2000) 'On the status of representations and derivations'. *University College London Working Papers in Linguistics* 12:343–65.

Brotherston, G. (1992) *Book of the Fourth World: Reading the Native Americas through their Literature.* Cambridge, Cambridge University Press.

Brown, C. and P. Hagoort (eds) (1999) *The Neurocognition of Language.* Oxford, Oxford University Press.

Cameron, D. (1995) *Verbal Hygiene.* London, Routledge.

Carruthers, P. and A. Chamberlain (eds) (2000) *Evolution and the Human Mind: Modularity, Language and Meta-cognition.* Cambridge, Cambridge University Press.

Cavalli-Sforza, L. L. (2000) *Genes, Peoples and Languages.* London, Allen Lane.

Chomsky, C. (1986) 'Analytic study of the Tadoma method: Language abilities of three deaf–blind subjects'. *Journal of Speech and Hearing Research* 29:332–47.

Chomsky, N. (1975) *Reflections on Language.* New York, Pantheon.

Chomsky, N. (1980) *Rules and Representations.* Oxford, Blackwell.

Chomsky, N. (1983) 'Interventionism and nuclear war'. In M. Albert and D. Dellinger (eds) *Beyond Survival: New Directions for the Disarmament Movement.* Boston, South End Press. Pp. 249–309.

Chomsky, N. (1991) 'Linguistics and adjacent fields: A personal view'. In A. Kasher (ed.) *The Chomskyan Turn.* Oxford, Blackwell. Pp. 3–25.

Chomsky, N. (1992) 'Explaining language use'. *Philosophical Topics* 20:205–31.

Chomsky, N. (1993a) 'Mental constructions and social reality'. In E. Reuland and W. Abraham (eds) *Knowledge and Language, Vol. 1: From Orwell's Problem to Plato's Problem.* Dordrecht, Kluwer. Pp. 29–58.

Chomsky, N. (1993b) *The Prosperous Few and the Restless Many.* Berkeley, CA, Odonian Press.

Chomsky, N. (1994a) 'Chomsky, Noam'. In S. Guttenplan (ed.) *A Companion to the Philosophy of Mind.* Blackwell, Oxford. Pp. 153–67.

Chomsky, N. (1994b) *Keeping the Rabble in Line: Interviews with David Barsamian.* Edinburgh, AK Press.

Chomsky, N. (1995a) 'Language and nature'. *Mind* 104:1–61.

Chomsky, N. (1995b) *The Minimalist Program.* Cambridge, MA, MIT Press.

Chomsky, N. (1996) *Powers and Prospects: Reflections on Human Nature and the Social Order.* London, Pluto Press.

Chomsky, N. (1998) *The Common Good: Interviews with David Barsamian.* Berkeley, CA, Odonian Press.

Chomsky, N. (1999a) 'Derivation by phase'. MS, MIT.

Chomsky, N. (1999b) 'Language and the brain'. MS, address at the European Conference on Cognitive Science, Siena.

Chomsky, N. (1999c) *Latin America: From Colonization to Globalization. In Conversation with Heinz Dieterich.* New York, Ocean Press.

Chomsky, N. (1999d) *The Umbrella of United States Power: The Universal Declaration of Human Rights and the Contradictions of United States Policy.* Open Media Pamphlet Series. New York, Seven Stories Press.

Chomsky, N. (1999e) *The New Military Humanism: Lessons from Kosovo.* Monroe, ME, Common Courage Press.

Chomsky, N. (1999f) *Fateful Triangle: The United States, Israel and the Palestinians.* Updated edition. London, Pluto Press.

Chomsky, N. (1999g) *Profit over People: Neoliberalism and Global Order.* New York, Seven Stories Press.

Chomsky, N. (2000a) *New Horizons in the Study of Language and Mind.* Cambridge, Cambridge University Press.

Chomsky, N. (2000b) 'Minimalist inquiries: The framework'. In R. Martin, D. Michaels and J. Uriagereka (eds) *Step by Step: Essays on Minimalist Syntax in Honor of Howard Lasnik.* Cambridge, MA, MIT Press. Pp. 89–155.

Chomsky, N. (2000c) 'States of concern'. In 'Manufacturing Monsters'; *Index on Censorship* 29,5:44–8.

Chomsky, N. (2000d) 'Foreign policy: The Colombian plan, April 2000'. *Z Magazine* 13,6:26–34.

Chomsky, N. (2000e) 'An interview on Minimalism' with Adriana Belletti and Luigi Rizzi. MS, University of Siena.

Chomsky, N. (2000f) *Rogue States: The Rule of Force in World Affairs.* London, Pluto Press.

Chomsky, N. and M. Halle (1968) *The Sound Pattern of English.* New York, Harper and Row.

Cole, J., G. Green and J. Morgan (eds) (1995) *Linguistics and Computation.* Stanford, CSLI.

Cole, R., J. Mariani, H. Uszkoreit, A. Zaenen and V. Zue (eds) (1997) *Linguistic Disorders and Pathologies: An International Handbook.* Berlin, Walter de Gruyter.

Collins, H. and T. Pinch (1993) *The Golem: What Everyone Should Know about Science.* Cambridge, Cambridge University Press.

Collins, H. and T. Pinch (1997) *The Golem at Large: What you Should Know about Technology.* Cambridge, Cambridge University Press.

Coltheart, M., R. Langdon and N. Breen (1997) 'Misidentification syndromes and cognitive neuropsychiatry'. *Trends in Cognitive Sciences* 1:157–8.

Corbett, G. and G. Morgan (1988) 'Colour terms in Russian: Reflections of typological constraints in a single language'. *Journal of Linguistics* 24:31–64.

Cormack, A. (1995a) 'The semantics of case'. *University College London Working Papers in Linguistics* 7:235–76.

Cormack, A. (1995b) 'On the treatment of attributive adjectives as adjuncts'. *Studia Linguistica* 49:93–6.

Cormack, A. (1999) 'Without specifiers'. In Adger et al. 1999:46–68.

Cormack, A. and R. Breheny (1994) 'Projections for functional categories'. *University College London Working Papers in Linguistics* 6:35–61.

Cormack, A. and N. Smith (1994) 'Serial verbs'. *University College London Working Papers in Linguistics* 6:63–88.

Cormack, A. and N. Smith (1996) 'Checking theory: Features, functional heads and checking parameters'. *University College London Working Papers in Linguistics* 8:243–81.

Cormack, A. and N. Smith (1997) 'Checking features and split signs'. *University College London Working Papers in Linguistics* 9:223–52.

Cormack, A. and N. Smith (1999) 'Why are depictives different from resultatives?'. *University College London Working Papers in Linguistics* 11:251–84.

Cormack, A. and N. Smith (2000) 'Head movement and negation in English'. *Transactions of the Philological Society* 98:49–85.

Coulmas, F. (ed.) (1997) *The Handbook of Sociolinguistics.* Oxford, Blackwell.

Crocker, M., M. Pickering and C. Clifton Jr (eds) (2000) *Architectures and Mechanisms for Language Processing*. Cambridge, Cambridge University Press.

Crystal, D. (1981) *Clinical Linguistics*. London, Whurr. 2nd edn 1989.

Crystal, D. (1982) *Profiling Linguistic Disability*. London, Edward Arnold.

Crystal, D. (1997) *The Cambridge Encyclopaedia of Language*. 2nd edn. Cambridge, Cambridge University Press.

Crystal, D. (2000) *Language Death*. Cambridge, Cambridge University Press.

Culicover, P. (1999) *Syntactic Nuts: Hard Cases, Syntactic Theory, and Language Acquisition*. Oxford, Oxford University Press.

Curcó Cobos, C. (1997) 'The pragmatics of humorous interpretations: A relevance-theoretic approach'. University College London PhD thesis.

Curcó (Cobos), C. (2000) 'Irony: Negation, echo and metarepresentation'. *Lingua* 110:257–80.

Curtiss, S. (1977) *Genie: A Psycholinguistic Study of a Modern-Day 'Wild Child'*. New York, Academic Press.

Davies, I., G. Corbett, A. Mtenje and P. Snowden (1995) 'The basic colour terms of Chichewa'. *Lingua* 95:259–78.

Dehaene, S. (1997) *The Number Sense*. London, Allen Lane.

Dennett, D. (1995) *Darwin's Dangerous Idea*. New York, Simon and Schuster.

Dixon, R. M. W. (1980) *The Languages of Australia*. Cambridge, Cambridge University Press.

Dunbar, R. and L. Barrett (2000) *Cousins: Our Primate Relatives*. London, BBC.

Duncan, A., R. Seitz, J. Kolodny, D. Bor, H. Herzog, A. Ahmed, F. Newell and H. Emslie (2000) 'A neural basis for general intelligence'. *Science* 289:457–60.

Duranti, A. (1997) *Linguistic Anthropology*. London, Cambridge University Press.

Elman, J. (1993) 'Learning and development in neural networks: the importance of starting small'. *Cognition* 48:71–99.

Elman, J., E. Bates, M. Johnson, A. Karmiloff-Smith, D. Parisi and K. Plunkett (1996) *Rethinking Innateness: A Connectionist Perspective on Development*. Cambridge, MA, MIT Press.

Eubank, L. and K. Gregg (forthcoming) 'Critical periods and (second) language acquisition'. To appear in D. Birdsong (ed.) *New Perspectives* on the Critical Period Hypothesis for Second Language Acquisition. Hillsdale, NJ, Lawrence Erlbaum.

Fabb, N. (1997) *Linguistics and Literature: Language in the Verbal Arts of the World.* Oxford, Blackwell.

Fabb, N. (in press) 'Weak monosyllables in iambic verse and the communication of metrical form'. *Lingua.*

Fitch, T. (2000) 'The evolution of speech: A comparative review'. *Trends in Cognitive Sciences* 4:258–67.

Fodor, J. (1975) *The Language of Thought.* New York, Crowell.

Fodor, J. (1983) *The Modularity of Mind.* Cambridge, MA, MIT Press.

Fodor, J. (1999) 'Diary'. *London Review of Books,* 30 September:68–9.

Fodor, J. (2000) *The Mind Doesn't Work That Way: The Scope and Limits of Computational Psychology.* Cambridge, MA, MIT Press.

Fodor, J. D. and F. Ferreira (eds) (1998) *Reanalysis in Sentence Processing.* Dordrecht, Kluwer.

Fowler, R. (1996) *Linguistic Criticism.* New York, Oxford University Press.

Franklin, S. (1989) 'Dissociations in auditory word comprehension'. *Aphasiology* 3:189–207.

Frith, U. (1989) *Autism: Explaining the Enigma.* Oxford, Blackwell.

Gazdar, G. (1980) 'A cross-categorial semantics for coordination'. *Linguistics and Philosophy* 3:407–9.

Gazzaniga, M. (ed.) (2000) *Cognitive Neuroscience: A Reader.* Oxford, Blackwell.

Gelman, R. and K. Brenneman (1994) 'First principles can support both universal and culture-specific learning about number and music'. In L. Hirschfeld and S. Gelman *Mapping the Mind: Domain Specificity in Cognition and Culture.* Cambridge, Cambridge University Press. Pp. 369–90.

Grossberg, S. (2000) 'The complementary brain: Unifying brain dynamics and modularity'. *Trends in Cognitive Sciences* 4:233–46.

Grunwell, P. (1987) *Clinical Phonology.* 2nd edn. London, Croom Helm.

Guttenplan, S. (ed.) (1994) *A Companion to the Philosophy of Mind.* Oxford, Blackwell.

Happé, F. (1999) 'Autism: Cognitive deficit or cognitive style?'. *Trends in Cognitive Sciences* 3,6:216–22.

Harley, T. (1996) *The Psychology of Language: From Data to Theory.* Psychology Press (Erlbaum).

Harris, R. A. (1993) *The Linguistics Wars.* Oxford, Oxford University Press.

Hauser, M. (2000) *Wild Minds: What Animals Really Think*. London, Penguin.

Herman, E. S. (1992) *Beyond Hypocrisy: Decoding the News in an Age of Propaganda*. Boston, South End Press.

Hernandez, A., A. Martinez and K. Kohnert (2000) 'In search of the language switch: An fMRI study of picture-naming in Spanish–English bilinguals'. *Brain and Language* 73:421–31.

Hock, H. H. (1991) *Principles of Historical Linguistics*. 2nd edn. Berlin, Mouton de Gruyter.

Howe, M. J. A. (1989) *Fragments of Genius*. London, Routledge.

Hudson, R. A. (1996) *Sociolinguistics*. 2nd edn. London, Cambridge University Press.

Isles, A. R. and L. S. Wilkinson (2000) 'Imprinted genes, cognition and behaviour'. *Trends in Cognitive Sciences* 4:309–18.

Jackendoff, R. (1999) 'Possible stages in the evolution of the language capacity'. *Trends in Cognitive Sciences* 3,7:272–9.

Jenkins, L. (2000) *Biolinguistics: Exploring the Biology of Language*. Cambridge, Cambridge University Press.

Johnson, K. and H. Johnson (eds) (1998) *Encyclopaedic Dictionary of Applied Linguistics*. Oxford, Blackwell.

Jusczyk, P. (1997) *The Discovery of Spoken Language*. Cambridge, MA, MIT Press.

Karmiloff-Smith, A. (1998) 'Development itself is the key to understanding developmental disorders'. *Trends in Cognitive Sciences* 2:389–98.

Kasher, A. (ed.) (1998) *Pragmatics: Critical Concepts*. 6 vol. London, Routledge.

Keller, H. (1903) *The Story of My Life: With Her Letters (1887–1901) and a Supplementary Account of Her Education, Including Passages from the Reports and Letters of Her Teacher, Anne Masefield Sullivan; by J. A. Macy*. London, Hodder and Stoughton.

Kim, K., N. Relkin, K.-M. Lee and J. Hirsch (1997) 'Distinct cortical areas associated with native and second languages'. *Nature* 388:171–4.

Knight, C., M. Studdert-Kennedy and J. Hurford (eds) (2000) *The Evolutionary Emergence of Language: Social Function and the Origins of Linguistic Form*. Cambridge, Cambridge University Press.

Kosslyn, S. (1994) *Image and Brain*. Cambridge, MA, MIT Press.

Kuhl, P. and J. Miller (1975) 'Speech perception by the chinchilla: Voiced–voiceless distinction in alveolar plosive consonants'. *Science* 190:69–72.

Lakatos, I. (1970) 'Falsification and the methodology of scientific research programmes'. In I. Lakatos and A. Musgrave (eds) *Criticism and the Growth of Knowledge*. Cambridge, Cambridge University Press. Pp. 91–195.

Lamarque, P. V. (ed.) (1997) *Concise Encyclopaedia of Philosophy of Language*. Oxford, Pergamon.

Landau, B. and L. Gleitman (1985) *Language and Experience: Evidence from the Blind Child*. Cambridge, MA, Harvard University Press.

Lenneberg, E. (1967) *Biological Foundations of Language*. New York, Wiley.

Lorenz, K. (1970) *Studies in Animal and Human Behaviour*. Vol. 1. London, Methuen.

McGilvray, J. (1994) 'Constant colors in the head'. *Synthese* 100:197–239.

Macken, M. (1980) 'The child's lexical representation: the *puzzle–puddle–pickle* evidence'. *Journal of Linguistics* 16:1–17.

MacLeod, C. M. (1991) 'Half a century of research on the Stroop Effect: An integrative review'. *Psychological Bulletin* 109:163–203.

MacLeod, C. M. and P. A. MacDonald (2000) 'Interdimensional interference in the Stroop effect: uncovering the cognitive and neural anatomy of attention'. *Trends in Cognitive Sciences* 4:383–91.

McMahon, A. (1994) *Understanding Language Change*. London, Cambridge University Press.

Martin, R. and J. Uriagereka (2000) 'Some possible foundations of the Minimalist Program'. In R. Martin, D. Michaels and J. Uriagereka (eds) *Step by Step: Essays on Minimalist Syntax in Honor of Howard Lasnik*. Cambridge, MA, MIT Press. Pp. 1–29.

Mayberry, R. (1993) 'First-language acquisition after childhood differs from second-language acquisition: The case of American Sign Language'. *Journal of Speech and Hearing Research* 36:1258–70.

Meyrink, G. (1928) *The Golem*. Boston, Houghton Mifflin.

Morgan, G., N. V. Smith, I.-M. Tsimpli and B. Woll (in press) 'Language against the odds: The learning of British Sign Language by a polyglot *savant*'. *Journal of Linguistics*.

Moss, A. E. (1989) 'Basic colour terms: Problems and hypotheses'. *Lingua* 78:313–20.

Motluk, A. (1995) 'How many people hear in colour?'. *New Scientist* 46,1979:18.

Nagel, T. (1997) *The Last Word*. Oxford, Oxford University Press.

Napoli, D. J. and J. Kegl (eds) (1991) *Bridges between Psychology and Linguistics: A Swarthmore Festschrift for Lila Gleitman.* Hillsdale, NJ, Lawrence Erlbaum.

Nichols, J. (1986) 'Head-marking and dependent-marking grammar'. *Language* 62:56–119.

Origgi, G. and D. Sperber (2000) 'Evolution, communication and the proper function of language'. In P. Carruthers and A. Chamberlain (eds) (2000) *Evolution and the Human Mind: Modularity, Language and Meta-cognition.* Cambridge, Cambridge University Press. Pp. 140–69.

Partee, B. H., A. ter Meulen and R. Wall (1993) *Mathematical Methods in Linguistics.* Dordrecht, Kluwer.

Payne, T. (1997) *Describing Morphosyntax: A Guide for Field Linguists.* Cambridge, Cambridge University Press.

Pinker, S. (1994) *The Language Instinct.* New York, William Morrow.

Pinker, S. (1999) *Words and Rules: The Ingredients of Language.* London, Weidenfeld and Nicolson.

Pinker, S. and P. Bloom (1990) 'Natural language and natural selection'. *Behavioral and Brain Sciences* 13:707–84.

Plotkin, H. (1998) *Evolution in Mind.* Cambridge, MA, Harvard University Press.

Polster, M. R. and S. Rose (1998) 'Disorders of auditory processing: Evidence for modularity in audition'. *Cortex* 34:47–65.

Povinelli, D. (2000) *Folk Physics for Apes.* Oxford, Oxford University Press.

Pullum, G. K. (1985) 'The linguistics of defamation'. *Natural Language and Linguistic Theory* 3:371–7.

Quartz, S. (1999) 'The constructivist brain'. *Trends in Cognitive Sciences* 3,2:48–57.

Raine, C. (1979) *A Martian Sends a Postcard Home.* Oxford, Oxford University Press.

Reed, C., W. Rabinowitz, N. Durlach, L. Braida, S. Conway-Fithian and M. Schultz (1985) 'Research on the Tadoma method of speech communication'. *Journal of the Acoustic Society of America* 77:247–57.

Reed, C., W. Rabinowitz, N. Durlach, L. Delhorne, L. Braida, J. Pemberton, B. Mulcahey and D. Washington (1992) 'Analytic study of the Tadoma method: Improving performance through the use of supplementary tactual displays'. *Journal of Speech and Hearing Research* 35:450–65.

Reed, C., L. Delhorne and N. Durlach (1995) 'A study of the tactual reception of Sign Language'. *Journal of Speech and Hearing Research* 38:477–89.

Renfrew, C. (1987) *Archaeology and Language: The Puzzle of Indo-European Origins.* Cambridge, Cambridge University Press.

Richardson, J. (1999) *Imagery.* Hove, Psychology Press.

Robertson, I. (1999) 'Cognitive rehabilitation: Attention and neglect'. *Trends in Cognitive Sciences* 3:385–93.

Rondal, J. (1995) *Exceptional Language Development in Down Syndrome.* Cambridge, Cambridge University Press.

Ross, J. R. (1967) 'Constraints on variables in syntax'. MIT PhD dissertation. Published (1986) as *Infinite Syntax.* Norwood, NJ, Ablex.

Rowson, M. (2000) 'Seriously funny'. *Index on Censorship* 29,6:23–9.

Rumelhart, D., J. McClelland and the PDP Research Group (1986) *Parallel Distributed Processing.* 2 vols. Cambridge, MA, MIT Press.

Sacks, O. (1985) *The Man Who Mistook His Wife for a Hat.* New York, Summit Books.

Santelmann, L. (1999) 'The acquisition of verb movement and Spec–Head relationships in child Swedish'. In Adger et al. 1999:271–98.

Savage-Rumbaugh, S., S. G. Shanker and T. J. Taylor (1998) *Apes, Language, and the Human Mind.* Oxford, Oxford University Press.

Schacter, D. L., E. Reiman, T. Curran, L. S. Yun, D. Bandy, K. B. McDermott and H. L. Roediger III (1996) 'Neuroanatomical correlates of veridical and illusory recognition memory: Evidence from Positron Emission Tomography'. *Neuron* 17:267–74.

Schlottmann, A. (2000) 'Is perception of causality modular?'. *Trends in Cognitive Sciences* 4:441–2.

Segal, G. (2000) *A Slim Book about Narrow Content.* Cambridge, MA, MIT Press.

Sieratzki, J. and B. Woll (in press) 'Toddling into language: Precocious language development in motor-impaired children with Spinal Muscular Atrophy'. *Lingua.*

Singer, I. B. (1983) *The Golem.* London, André Deutsch.

Sloboda, J. (1985) *The Musical Mind: The Cognitive Psychology of Music.* Oxford, Clarendon Press.

Smith, N. V. (1964) 'A phonological and grammatical study of the verb in Nupe'. UCL, University of London, PhD thesis.

Smith, N. V. (1973) *The Acquisition of Phonology: A Case Study.* Cambridge, Cambridge University Press.

Smith, N. V. (1978) 'Lexical representation and the acquisition of phonology'. In B. Kachru (ed.) *Linguistics in the Seventies: Directions and Prospects*. Special Issue, *Studies in the Linguistic Sciences* 8:259–73.

Smith, N. V. (1989) *The Twitter Machine*. Oxford, Blackwell.

Smith, N. V. (1999) *Chomsky: Ideas and Ideals*. Cambridge, Cambridge University Press.

Smith, N. V. (2001) 'Singing by the dead'. *Glot International* 5:000–000.

Smith, N. V. (in press) 'Dissociation and modularity: Reflections on language and mind'. In M. Banich and M. Mack (eds) *Mind, Brain and Language*. Hillsdale, NJ, Lawrence Erlbaum.

Smith, N. V. and I.-M. Tsimpli (1995) *The Mind of a Savant: Language Learning and Modularity*. Oxford, Blackwell.

Smith, N. V. and D. Wilson (1979) *Modern Linguistics: The Results of Chomsky's Revolution*. Harmondsworth, Penguin.

Smith, N. V., I.-M. Tsimpli and J. Ouhalla (1993) 'Learning the impossible: The acquisition of possible and impossible languages by a polyglot *savant*'. *Lingua* 91:279–47.

Spelke, E. and S. Tsivkin (2001) 'Initial knowledge and conceptual change: Space and number'. In M. Bowerman and S. Levinson (eds) *Language Acquisition and Conceptual Development*. Cambridge, Cambridge University Press. Pp. 70–97.

Sperber, D. (1985) 'Apparently irrational beliefs'. In D. Sperber *On Anthropological Knowledge*. Cambridge, Cambridge University Press. Pp. 35–63.

Sperber, D. (1994a) 'Understanding verbal understanding'. In J. Khalfa (ed.) *What is Intelligence?*. Cambridge, Cambridge University Press. Pp. 179–98.

Sperber, D. (1994b) 'The modularity of thought and the epidemiology of representations'. In L. Hirschfeld and S. Gelman (eds) *Mapping the Mind: Domain Specificity in Cognition and Culture*. Cambridge, Cambridge University Press. Pp. 39–67.

Sperber, D. and D. Wilson (1995) *Relevance: Communication and Cognition*. 2nd edn. Oxford, Blackwell.

Steedman, M. (1997) *Surface Structure and Interpretation*. Cambridge, MA, MIT Press.

Sternberg, R. J. (2000) 'The holey grail of general intelligence'. *Science* 289:399–401.

Suga, N. (1995) 'Processing of auditory information carried by species-specific complex sounds'. In M. Gazzaniga (ed.) *The Cognitive Neurosciences*. Cambridge, MA, MIT Press. Pp. 295–313.

Sunshine, L. (ed.) (1993) *The Illustrated Woody Allen Reader*. London, Jonathan Cape.

Sutton-Spence, R. L. and B. Woll (1999) *An Introduction to the Linguistics of BSL*. Cambridge, Cambridge University Press.

Swinney, D. (1979) 'Lexical access during sentence comprehension: (Re)consideration of context effects'. *Journal of Verbal Learning and Verbal Behavior* 18:645–59.

Tager-Flusberg, H. (ed.) (1999) *Neurodevelopmental Disorders*. Cambridge, MA, MIT Press.

Tannen, D. (1989) *Talking Voices: Repetition, Dialogue, and Imagery in Conversational Discourse*. Cambridge, Cambridge University Press.

Thompson, D'A. W. (1942) *On Growth and Form*. 2 vols. Cambridge, Cambridge University Press.

Tomasello, M. and J. Call (1997) *Primate Cognition*. Oxford, Oxford University Press.

Tsimpli, I.-M. and N. V. Smith (1995) 'Minds, maps and modules: Evidence from a polyglot savant'. *Working Papers of the Cambridge Research Centre for English and Applied Linguistics* 2:1–25.

Tsimpli, I.-M. and N. V. Smith (1998) 'Modules and quasi-modules'. *Learning and Individual Differences* 10:193–215.

Van der Berghe, P. L. (1983) 'Human inbreeding avoidance: Culture in nature'. *Behavioral and Brain Sciences* 6:91–123.

Van der Lely, H. K. J. (1997) 'Language and cognitive development in a grammatical SLI boy: Modularity and innateness'. *Journal of Neurolinguistics* 10:75–107.

Vargha-Khadem, F., L. Carr, E. Isaacs, E. Brett, C. Adams and M. Mishkin (1997) 'Onset of speech after left hemispherectomy in a nine-year-old boy'. *Brain* 120:159–82.

Varley, R. and M. Siegal (2000) 'Evidence for cognition without grammar from causal reasoning and "theory of mind" in an agrammatic aphasic patient'. *Current Biology* 10:723–6.

Warrington, E. K. (1984) *Recognition Memory Test*. London, NFER-Nelson.

Wilson, D. (1995) 'Is there a maxim of truthfulness?'. *UCL Working Papers in Linguistics* 7:197–212.

Wilson, D. and N. Smith (eds) (1992) *Relevance Theory*. Special issue of *Lingua*, 87,1/2.

Index

Bold type indicates that the item has an entry in the glossary.

acquisition of language 26,
41, 49–52, 76, 83, 85, 87,
95–9, 105–6, 114
agnosia 35–6
Ainu 30
alliteration 120
Amahl 49–52, 117
ambiguity 3, 16, 33, 93, 107
American Sign Language *see*
ASL
amusia 36
anthropology 7
aphasia 6, 34, 36, 41, 96–7,
106
applied linguistics 72
apraxia 24
archaeology 8, 73
artificial intelligence 6
ASL 14–15, 98
association 106–7, 109
see also memory
autism 18–22, 24, 62

babies 37
background 60
bats 37

behaviourism 85, 110
Bellugi, Ursula 42
bilingualism 6, 98–9
biology 5, 89
blindness 13–17, 29, 40, 98
bonobos 3, 83–8
Borsley, Bob 72
brain 5–6, 17, 34–7, 43–4,
89, 92–3, 97–8, 111, 114
British Sign Language *see* BSL
Broca's area 98
Brody, Misi 71
BSL 23, 26
Burge, Tyler 103

calendrical calculators 20, 42
Cameron, Deborah 53, 55
cancellability 9
Capgras' Delusion 40–1
categorial perception 34,
37–8, 86
censorship 54–7
central system 28, 30–3, 38,
40–1, 44, 63
cerebral dominance 5–6,
36–7, 114

chess 6
Chichewa 30
chimpanzees *see* bonobos
chinchillas 37, 86
Chomsky, Carol 14
Chomsky, Noam 26–7, 62,
 71–3, 89–94, 100–4, 105,
 112, *et passim*
Christopher 19–23, 24–7,
 42–3, 99, 108
Coleridge 40, 44
Collins, Harry 69–74
colour 13, 28–33
communication 3, 15, 18, 22,
 84, 86–7, 103
competence 49 *see also*
 I-language
complementation 79
computational linguistics 7
conjunction 16, 75–80
connectionism 105–9,
 110–15, 120
conservation 19, 24–5, 42
consonant harmony 51, 119
constructivism 93–4
control 16
coordination *see* conjunction
Cormack, Annabel 76–80
critical period 95–9
Curcó, Carmen 58–62
Curtiss, Sue 97

deafness 13–17, 36–7, 40,
 98
de Bernières, Louis 63, 65
decoding 22, 93
deep structure 89, 96
Dehaene, Stanislas 42
Dennett, Daniel 90
depictives 79

dissociation (modular) 20,
 34–7, 40–5, 86, 99
dissociation (pragmatic) 60
domain-specificity 38, 86, 112
Down syndrome 42, 97–8

E-language 85–6, 102–3
Einstein, Albert 70, 72
ellipsis 93
empty categories 71, 75–6,
 80
etymology 117
evolution 8, 68, 89–94, 95
expressive power 28–9
externalism *see* E-language

Fabb, Nigel 73
face recognition 42
false belief 19, 21, 25, 87
falsifiability 69, 71, 73–4, 120
Fibonacci series 91
Fodor, Jerry 28, 30, 40, 44,
 87, 93
foreground 60
forensic linguistics 8
Frege 102
frequency 108, 113
functional categories 75–6,
 99, 111

Galileo 90
Gazdar, Gerald 71
genetics 4, 90–1, 96, 99, 108,
 112
Genie *see* wolf children
German 108
Golem 69–74

haemophilia 40
Hale, Ken 96

Hiroshima 70
historical linguistics 8, 106,
  117
'human' 3, 13
humour 58–62

I-language 85, 101
imagery 63–8
imaging 5–6, 41, 44, 98, 106
imprinting 95
incest 38, 95
inference 59, 86–7, 93
infinity 92
informational encapsulation
  30–2, 44
Ingham, Richard 72
innateness 4, 71, 86–7,
  89–90, 96, 112, 114–15, 117
input systems *see* modularity
intelligence 24–7, 41–2, 45,
  84, 86–8
internalism 89, 102–4
  see also I-language
interpretive use 61
intersective adjectives 79
intonation 16, 76
invented language 26–7, 108
irony 21, 61
irregularity 106–9

jackdaws 95–9
Jenkins, Lyle 89–94
jokes 21, 53, 59, 61–2
Jusczyk, Peter 99

Karmiloff-Smith, Annette 43
Keller, Helen 14, 17, 98
knowledge of language 4, 9,
  89

language acquisition *see*
  acquisition of language
language death 8
language of thought 87
law 8, 73
learnability 71, 105, 110, 112
Lenneberg, Eric 97
lexicon 20, 26, 43, 86, 99
libel 8
loan-words 108
Locke 13
London 101–2
Lorenz, Konrad 95
lying 25, 61

machine translation 6
mathematics 7, 42–3
maturation 110–11
Mayberry, Rachel 14, 98
meaning *see* semantics
memory 33, 35, 42, 44,
  106–9, 111
metalinguistic negation 21
metaphor 21
metarepresentation 21,
  61–2, 67
metrics 7
minimalism 89
mistakes 51
modularity 19, 27, 28–33,
  36, 38, 40, 42–4, 63, 85–6,
  93, 112, 114
Montague, Richard 72
moral judgement 38, 86
morphology 20, 43, 99
movement *see* transformations
Mueller-Lyer illusion 31–2
mushrooms 90, 93
music 34–5, 37–8

natural selection 90–2
negation 16, 21, 75–6
neologisms 107–8
networks *see* connectionism
neurolinguistics 6
neurology 5
noise 34–9
'normal' 43
normativity 56
number 29, 33, 92
Nupe 8, 80

onomasiology 116–20
operator 75–80
owls 37

palatography 15
parametric variation 20, 26,
34–5, 37–8, 79–80, 87, 90,
99
parasitic gaps 25, 115
perception 13–16, 34–9, 51
Pesetsky, David 33
PET scan *see* imaging
phonagnosia 36
phonology 49–52, 63, 76,
99, 116–20
Piaget, Jean 41
Pinch, Trevor 69–74
Pinker, Steven 90, 93, 105–9
plasticity 114
poverty of the stimulus 111,
114–15
pragmatics 9, 63, 67, 86, 104
see also Relevance Theory
pre-functional stage 85
pretence 21–2, 83, 87
priming 32, 107
primitive languages 4

principles and parameters
see parametric variation,
universals
pro-drop 20, 26
pronominalization 16
pronunciation 49–52
prosopagnosia 36, 40–1
prototypes 109
psychology 4, 89
public language *see* E-language
Putnam, Hilary 103

quasi-modules 38, 112

racism 53, 56–7
Rainman 20
rationalism 107
rationality 56
reductionism 111
reference 100–4
regularity 106–9
relativity 70
relevance 9, 64–6
Relevance Theory 18, 58,
64–7, 73
resemblance 65
resultatives 79
retreat 114
rhetorical questions 21
Rimbaud 28
Ross, J. R. (Haj) 78
rules 50, 105–9, 110
Russian 30

Sacks, Oliver 36, 40
'Sally-Anne' 18–20
Savage-Rumbaugh, Sue 83–8
savants 19–20, 25
Schacter, Daniel 44

scepticism 100–1
semantics 6, 16, 35, 79, 101–4
serial verbs 78, 80
seriation 42
sexism 53–7
Shebalin 34, 41
sign language 13–17, 98
SLI 43
Smarties 19–20
sociolinguistics 7
sociology 7, 72
speciesism 86, 88
Specific Language Impairment see SLI
speech therapy 6, 73
Sperber, Dan 61, 67
spinal muscular atrophy 43
sruti 38
strokes 5
Stroop effect 30–2
structure dependence 27, 85, 108, 113–14
style 7
subordination 75–80
sunflowers 90–1
Swinney, David 33
synaesthesia 28–33
syntax 6, 20, 26, 43, 63, 84–7, 97, 99, 104, 110–15

Tadoma 13–17, 98
Tadzhik 80
tag questions 16
that-trace 20

Theory of Mind 18, 21, 62, 83, 86–7
Tokaimura 70
transformations 71, 79
. tion 21, 26
triggering 38, 90
truth 65–8, 69–70, 89, 100–1
Tsimpli, Ianthi 19, 27, 62, 99, 108
twin-earth 103

UG 26, 28, 85
unbounded dependencies 71
underspecification 120
unification 73, 92
universal grammar see UG
universals 4, 28, 38, 51–2, 79–80, 90, 110–11, 120

visual perception 29
vocabulary 20, 25, 29, 42–3, 84, 87, 97, 103
Voice Onset Time see VOT
VOT 37–8, 86

whales 90–1
wh-island 20
Williams syndrome 42
Wilson, Deirdre 65, 67
see also Relevance Theory
Wittgenstein 63, 65, 85
wolf children 97
Woody Allen 58–62

Zangwill, Oliver 35

CPSIA information can be obtained
at www.ICGtesting.com
Printed in the USA
BVOW04s1721211216

471422BV00006B/74/P